PASSPORT BOOKS

FRENCH PICTURE DICTIONARY

Angela Wilkes
Illustrated by Colin King
Translated by Katherine Folliot

Consultant: Betty Root

Fifi   Mimi   Sam Strongman   The dogs   Grandpa

Aa

actor — l'acteur (m)[1]

Voici un acteur célèbre.
This is a famous actor.

afternoon — l'après-midi (m)

Viens me voir cet après-midi.
Come and see me this afternoon.

Il fait du football l'après-midi.
He plays soccer in the afternoon.

about — sur

Voici un livre sur les dragons.
This is a book about dragons.

to add — ajouter

Aggie ajoute du sucre au thé.
Aggie adds sugar to the tea.

again — encore

Henri a eu encore un accident.
Henry has had an accident again.

above — au-dessus de

Le cerf-volant vole au-dessus de l'arbre.
The kite is flying above the tree.

address — l'adresse (f)

Voici l'adresse d'Henri.
This is Henry's address.

against — contre

Fifi s'appuie contre un mur.
Fifi is leaning against a wall.

accident — l'accident (m)

Henri a un accident.
Henry has an accident.

to be afraid — avoir peur

Le chien a peur des souris.
The dog is afraid of mice.

age — l'âge (m)

Ces hommes ont le même âge.
These men are the same age.

across — à travers

Le chien court à travers le parc.
The dog runs across the park.

after — après

Mardi vient après lundi.
Tuesday comes after Monday.

Il est arrivé après minuit.
He arrived after midnight.

Le chien court après le chat.
The dog runs after the cat.

air — l'air (m)

L'avion est en l'air.
The airplane is in the air.

1. actress: l'actrice (f)

| airplane | l'avion (m) | alone | seul | always | toujours |

Cet avion est vert.
This airplane is green.

Fifi est toute seule.
Fifi is all alone.

Henri a toujours des accidents.
Henry always has accidents.

| airport | l'aéroport (m) | along | le long de | ambulance | l'ambulance (f) |

Le pilote voit l'aéroport.
The pilot sees the airport.

Des fleurs poussent le long du chemin.
Flowers grow along the path.

L'ambulance arrive.
The ambulance is arriving.

| alarm clock | le réveil | alphabet | l'alphabet (m) | among | parmi |

Le réveil sonne.
The alarm clock is ringing.

Toutes ces lettres sont dans l'alphabet.
All these letters are in the alphabet.

Le chat se cache parmi les oiseaux.
The cat is hiding among the birds.

| all | tous, toutes | already | déjà | and | et |

Toutes les souris sont roses.
All the mice are pink.

Mimi a déjà un petit gâteau.
Mimi already has a cupcake.

Voici Fritz et Hank.
Here are Fritz and Hank.

| almost | presque | also | aussi | angel | l'ange (m) |

Il a presque fini.
He has almost finished.

Mimi est une fille; c'est aussi un bébé.
Mimi is a girl; she is also a baby.

Fifi n'est pas seulement belle, elle est aussi intelligente.
Fifi is not only beautiful, she is also smart.

L'ange vole.
The angel is flying.

5

angry	en colère

L'ange est en colère.
The angel is angry.

animal	l'animal (m)

Ce sont tous des animaux.*
These are all animals.

another	un/une autre

Bill prend un autre petit gâteau.
Bill takes another cupcake.

answer	la solution[1]

**Voici une addition et sa
solution.**
Here is an addition problem and
the answer to it.

ant	la fourmi

La fourmi court sur le livre.
The ant runs over the book.

any	des

Avez-vous des oeufs?
Do you have any eggs?

anybody	quelqu'un

Y a-t-il quelqu'un ici?
Is anybody there?

apartment	l'appartement (m)

**Fifi habite dans un
appartement.**
Fifi lives in an apartment.

apple	la pomme

Fifi mange une pomme.
Fifi is eating an apple.

apron	le tablier

Bill met son tablier.
Bill puts on his apron.

to argue	se disputer

Bill et Ben se disputent.
Bill and Ben are arguing.

arm	le bras

Ben a le bras cassé.
Ben has a broken arm.

army	l'armée (f)

Bill est dans l'armée.
Bill is in the army.

to arrange	arranger

**Fifi arrange les fleurs dans un
vase.**
Fifi arranges the flowers in a vase.

to arrive	arriver

Le train arrive.
The train arrives.

arrow	la flèche

**Sherlock Holmes trouve une
flèche.**
Sherlock Holmes finds an arrow.

1. The word for an answer to a question is **la réponse**.

artist	l'artiste (m ou f)	aunt	la tante	back	le dos

L'artiste peint.
The artist is painting.

Tante Aggie est la soeur de maman.
Aunt Aggie is Mom's sister.

Henri se gratte le dos.
Henry scratches his back.

---

as   **lorsque**

Il pleuvait lorsque nous sommes partis.
It was raining as we left.

as . . . as   **aussi . . . que**

Max est aussi intelligent que Ruff.
Max is as smart as Ruff.

(to take) away   **emporter**

Le vent emporte le journal de Ben.
The wind takes Ben's newspaper away.

---

bad   **mauvais**

Il fait mauvais aujourd'hui.
The weather is bad today.

Papa est de mauvaise humeur.
Dad is in a bad mood.

Elle a un mauvais rhume.
She has a bad cold.

---

to ask (for)   **demander**

Mimi demande une pomme.
Mimi asks for an apple.

---

bag   **le sac**

Le sac est plein d'argent.
The bag is full of money.

---

astronaut   **l'astronaute (m)**

Voici un astronaute.
Here is an astronaut.

baby   **le bébé**

Le bébé pleure.
The baby is crying.

---

baker   **le boulanger**

Le boulanger fait le pain.
The baker makes bread.

---

at   **à, au**

À quatre heures nous prenons le thé.
At four o'clock we have tea.

Les enfants sont à l'école et Ben est au travail.
The children are at school and Ben is at work.

---

baby carriage   **le landau**

Mimi est dans un landau.
Mimi is in a baby carriage.

---

ball   **le ballon**[1]

Max attrape le ballon.
Max catches the ball.

---

1. **Le ballon** is the word used for a big ball. A small ball is **la balle.**

balloon	**le ballon**

Mimi joue avec un ballon.
Mimi plays with a balloon.

banana	**la banane**

Un gros régime de bananes.*
A big bunch of bananas.

band	**la fanfare**

La fanfare joue.
The band is playing.

bank	**le bord**

Jim est au bord de la rivière.
Jim is on the river bank.

bank	**la banque**

Fred quitte la banque en courant.
Fred runs away from the bank.

---

to bark	**aboyer**

Le chien aboie.
The dog is barking.

baseball	**le baseball**

Henri joue au baseball.
Henry is playing baseball.

basket	**le panier**

Le panier est plein de pommes.
The basket is full of apples.

bathroom	**la salle de bains**

La baignoire est dans la salle de bains.
The bathtub is in the bathroom.

bathtub	**la baignoire**

Le chat est dans la baignoire.
The cat is in the bathtub.

---

beach	**la plage**

Fifi est allongée sur la plage.
Fifi is lying on the beach.

beak	**le bec**

L'oiseau a un bec rouge.
The bird has a red beak.

bean	**le haricot**

Voici des haricots* verts.
These are green beans.

bear	**l'ours (m)**

Bruno est un ours brun.
Bruno is a brown bear.

beard	**la barbe**

Cet homme a une longue barbe.
This man has a long beard.

beautiful — beau, belle

Une belle princesse.
A beautiful princess.

because — parce que

Le bébé pleure parce qu'il a faim.
The baby is crying because it is hungry.

Il est gros parce qu'il mange trop.
He is fat because he eats too much.

bed — le lit

Le roi est au lit.
The king is in bed.

bedroom — la chambre

Le lit est dans la chambre.
The bed is in the bedroom.

bee — l'abeille (f)

L'abeille est sur une fleur.
The bee is on a flower.

beef — le boeuf

Bob coupe le rôti de boeuf.
Bob is slicing the roast beef.

before — avant

Lundi vient avant mardi.
Monday comes before Tuesday.

Il est arrivé avant minuit.
He arrived before midnight.

Bill se lève avant Ben.
Bill gets up before Ben.

to begin — commencer

Il commence à pleuvoir.
It is beginning to rain.

Le match commence.
The game is beginning.

Le film commence à sept heures.
The movie begins at seven o'clock.

behind — derrière

Qui est derrière l'arbre?
Who is behind the tree?

to believe — croire

Sam croit à mon histoire.
Sam believes my story.

Sam croit tout ce qu'on lui dit.
Sam believes anything you tell him.

Papy croit en Dieu.
Grandpa believes in God.

bell — la cloche

La cloche sonne.
The bell is ringing.

bellboy — le porteur

Un porteur porte des valises.
A bellboy carries suitcases.

to belong to — appartenir à

Le chapeau appartient à Ben.
The hat belongs to Ben.

À qui ceci appartient-il?
Who does this belong to?

Ceci appartient à Fifi.
It belongs to Fifi.

below — au-dessous de

Le chat est deux marches au-dessous de Bruno.
The cat is two stairs below Bruno.

belt — la ceinture

Fifi porte une grosse ceinture.
Fifi is wearing a big belt.

bench	le banc

L'oiseau est sur le banc.
The bird is on the bench.

to bend	plier

Sam fait plier une cuiller.
Sam is bending a spoon.

best	le meilleur
	la meilleure

Fifi est la meilleure danseuse.
Fifi is the best dancer.

Il est le meilleur de la classe.
He is the best in the class.

better	mieux

Fifi danse mieux que Susie.
Fifi dances better than Susie.

Henri parle mieux le français que Ben.
Henry speaks French better than Ben.

between	entre

Le chat est entre les deux ours.
The cat is between the two bears.

bicycle	la bicyclette

Le boulanger est sur sa bicyclette.
The baker is on his bicycle.

big	gros, grosse

L'éléphant est gros.
The elephant is big.

bird	l'oiseau (m)

L'oiseau est perché sur une bicyclette.
The bird is perched on a bicycle.

birthday	l'anniversaire (m)

C'est aujourd'hui l'anniversaire de Mimi.
Today is Mimi's birthday.

to bite	mordre

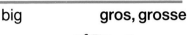

Le chien mord le facteur.
The dog bites the mailman.

black	noir

Le gros chat est noir.
The big cat is black.

blackbird	le merle

Un merle est noir.
A blackbird is black.

blackboard	le tableau noir

Ben dessine au tableau noir.
Ben draws on the blackboard.

blanket	la couverture

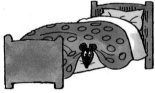

Il y a une couverture rouge sur le lit.
There is a red blanket on the bed.

blind man	l'aveugle
blind woman	(m ou f)

Un chien guide l'aveugle.
A dog leads the blind man.

| blond **blond** | body **le corps** | boot **la botte** |

L'ami de Fifi a les cheveux blonds.
Fifi's friend has blond hair.

Un corps puissant.
A strong body.

Cet oiseau a une botte bleue.
This bird has a blue boot.

| blood **le sang** | bone **l'os (m)** | both **les deux** |

Sam a du sang sur le doigt.
Sam has blood on his finger.

Fluff a un gros os.
Fluff has a big bone.

Les deux cochons sont roses.
Both the pigs are pink.

| to blow out **souffler** | bonfire **le feu de joie** | bottle **la bouteille** |

Mimi souffle les bougies.
Mimi blows out the candles.

Le feu de joie est en train de brûler.
The bonfire is burning.

Une grande bouteille de vin.
A big bottle of wine.

| blue **bleu** | book **le livre** | bottom **le bas** |

La maison est bleue.
The house is blue.

Voici un livre sur les bateaux.
This is a book about boats.

La grenouille est en bas de l'échelle.
The frog is at the bottom of the ladder.

| boat **le bateau** | bookstore **la librairie** | bowl **la coupe** |

Trois hommes dans un bateau.
Three men in a boat.

Bill va à la librairie.
Bill goes to the bookstore.

Une coupe pleine de bananes.
A bowl full of bananas.

box **la boîte**	to break **casser**	bridgeroom **le marié**

box **la boîte**

Le chat dort dans une boîte.
The cat sleeps in a box.

to break **casser**

Ben casse le pain.
Ben breaks the bread.

bridegroom **le marié**

Et son marié.
And the bridegroom.

boy **le garçon**

Tom est un petit garçon.
Tom is a little boy.

breakfast **le petit déjeuner**

Fifi prend son petit déjeuner.
Fifi has her breakfast.

bridge **le pont**

Bill traverse le pont.
Bill crosses the bridge.

bracelet **le bracelet**

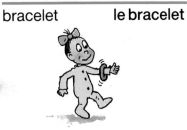

Mimi porte un bracelet bleu.
Mimi is wearing a blue bracelet.

to breathe **respirer**

Les poissons respirent sous l'eau.
Fish breathe underwater.

bright **brillant**

Une étoile brillante.
A bright star.

branch **la branche**

L'oiseau est sur la branche.
The bird is on the branch.

brick **la brique**

L'homme porte une brique.
The man is carrying a brick.

to bring **apporter**

Max apporte une pantoufle à Bill.
Max brings Bill a slipper.

bread **le pain**

Bill coupe le pain.
Bill cuts the bread.

bride **la mariée**

Une belle mariée.
A beautiful bride.

brother **le frère**

Bill et Ben sont frères. *
Bill and Ben are brothers.

brown **brun**	to build **construire**	bump **la bosse**

Bruno est un ours brun.
Bruno is a brown bear.

L'homme construit une maison.
The man is building a house.

Henri heurte une bosse.
Henry hits a bump.

brush **la brosse**	building **le bâtiment**	bunch **le bouquet**

Fritz se nettoie les chaussures avec une brosse.
Fritz cleans his shoes with a brush.

Une maison est un bâtiment.
A house is a building.

Un gros bouquet de fleurs.
A big bunch of flowers.

bubble **la bulle**	bulb **le bulbe**	burglar **le cambrioleur**

L'ours fait une bulle.
The bear blows a bubble.

Une chenille regarde le bulbe.
A caterpillar looks at the bulb.

Le cambrioleur se sauve.
The burglar runs away.

bucket **le seau**	bull **le taureau**	to burn **brûler**

Bill vide le seau.
Bill empties the bucket.

Le taureau poursuit Bill.
The bull chases Bill.

La maison brûle.
The house is burning.

bud **le bourgeon**	bulldozer **le bulldozer**	bus **l'autobus (m)**

La plante a un bourgeon.
The plant has one bud.

Ben conduit un bulldozer.
Ben drives a bulldozer.

L'autobus s'arrête.
The bus is stopping.

bus stop　l'arrêt d'autobus (m)

Fifi attend à l'arrêt d'autobus.
Fifi waits at the bus stop.

bush　le buisson

Qui est derrière le buisson?
Who is behind the bush?

busy　occupé

Cet homme est très occupé.
This man is very busy.

but　mais

Bill mange beaucoup mais il n'est pas gros.
Bill eats a lot but he is not fat.

J'aime les bonbons mais pas le chocolat.
I like candy but I do not like chocolate.

butcher　le boucher

Le boucher vend de la viande.
The butcher sells meat.

butter　le beurre

Le beurre fond.
The butter is melting.

butterfly　le papillon

Un papillon sur une fleur.
A butterfly on a flower.

button　le badge

Bill porte beaucoup de badges. *
Bill is wearing many buttons.

to buy　acheter

Fifi achète des bananes.
Fifi buys some bananas.

by　à côté de

L'homme est à côté de la voiture.
The man is by the car.

C c

cabbage　le chou

Fifi choisit un chou.
Fifi picks out a cabbage.

café　le café

Les amis vont au café.
The friends go to a café.

cage　la cage

Le lion est dans une cage.
The lion is in a cage.

cake　le gâteau

Fifi coupe le gâteau.
Fifi cuts the cake.

14

calculator	**la calculatrice**	camera	**l'appareil-photo**	capital	**la capitale**

L'homme se sert de sa calculatrice.
The man uses his calculator.

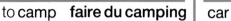

Bill a un nouvel appareil-photo.
Bill has a new camera.

Rome est la capitale de l'Italie.
Rome is the capital of Italy.

Paris est la capitale de la France.
Paris is the capital of France.

---

calendar	**le calendrier**	to camp	**faire du camping**	car	**la voiture**

Aggie regarde le calendrier.
Aggie looks at the calendar.

Bill et Ben font du camping.
Bill and Ben are camping.

Fred conduit une voiture rapide.
Fred drives a fast car.

---

calf	**le veau**	candle	**la bougie**	card	**la carte**

Un veau avec sa mère.
A calf with its mother.

Henri porte une bougie.
Henry is carrying a candle.

Un jeu de cartes. *
A game of cards.

---

to call	**appeler**	candy	**le bonbon**	carpet	**le tapis**

Le fermier appelle le veau.
The farmer calls the calf.

Mimi mange des bonbons. *
Mimi is eating candy.

Le tapis est bleu.
The carpet is blue.

---

camel	**le chameau**	cap	**la casquette**	carrot	**la carotte**

Henri monte sur un chameau.
Henry is riding a camel.

Fred porte une casquette.
Fred is wearing a cap.

Une botte de carottes. *
A bunch of carrots.

to carry	porter[1]

Mimi porte des carottes.
Mimi is carrying carrots.

cauliflower	le chou-fleur

Un chou-fleur dans un panier.
A cauliflower in a basket.

chair	la chaise

Bruno est assis sur une chaise.
Bruno is sitting on a chair.

castle	le château

Le château est sur une colline.
The castle is on a hill.

cave	la caverne

Il y a un trésor dans la caverne.
There is treasure in the cave.

chalk	la craie

Bruno écrit avec de la craie.
Bruno is writing with chalk.

cat	le chat[2]

Le chat est sur le tapis.
The cat is on the carpet.

ceiling	le plafond

Sam touche le plafond.
Sam touches the ceiling.

change	la monnaie

Bill compte sa monnaie.
Bill counts his change.

to catch	attraper

Le chat attrape le ballon.
The cat is catching the ball.

cellar	la cave

La cave est pleine de bouteilles.
The cellar is full of bottles.

to change	changer

Henri change une roue.
Henry changes a tire.

caterpillar	la chenille

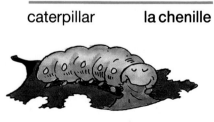

La chenille mange une feuille.
The caterpillar is eating a leaf.

chain	la chaîne

La montre est attachée à une chaîne.
The watch is on a chain.

to chase	poursuivre

Henri poursuit un voleur.
Henry chases a thief.

1. **porter** also means "to wear."   2. a female cat: **la chatte**

cheap **bon marché**	**chest** **la poitrine**	**chimpanzee** **le chimpanzé**

cheap   **bon marché**

Ce fauteuil est bon marché.
This easy chair is cheap.

chest   **la poitrine**

Sam se frappe la poitrine.
Sam is beating his chest.

chimpanzee   **le chimpanzé**

Un chimpanzé dans un arbre.
A chimpanzee in a tree.

check   **le chèque**

Bill fait un chèque.
Bill writes a check.

chick   **le poussin**

La poule a cinq poussins. *
The hen has five chicks.

chin   **le menton**

Sam se frotte le menton.
Sam rubs his chin.

cheek   **la joue**

Mamie a les joues* roses.
Grandma has pink cheeks.

chicken   **le poulet**

Ben découpe le poulet.
Ben is cutting the chicken.

chocolate   **le chocolat**

Mimi mange du chocolat.
Mimi is eating chocolate.

cheese   **le fromage**

Fifi mange du fromage.
Fifi is eating cheese.

child   **l'enfant (m)**

Les enfants* jouent.
The children are playing.

to choose   **choisir**

Fifi choisit une robe verte.
Fifi chooses a green dress.

cherry   **la cerise**

Un oiseau mange les cerises. *
A bird is eating the cherries.

chimney   **la cheminée**

L'oiseau est sur la cheminée.
The bird is on the chimney.

chop   **la côtelette**

Ben mange une côtelette de porc.
Ben is eating a pork chop.

Christmas — **Noël**	class — **la classe**	cliff — **la falaise**

C'est Noël.
It is Christmas.

Il y a cinq enfants dans la classe.
There are five children in the class.

Henri est sur une falaise.
Henry is on a cliff.

church — **l'église (f)**	classroom — **la classe**	to climb up — **escalader**

Fifi va à l'église.
Fifi goes to church.

La classe est vide.
The classroom is empty.

Sam escalade la falaise.
Sam is climbing up the cliff.

circle — **le cercle**	clean — **propre**	clock — **l'horloge (f)**

Les poussins forment un cercle.
The chicks are running in a circle.

Bill met un tablier propre.
Bill puts on a clean apron.

Ben nettoie l'horloge.
Ben is cleaning the clock.

circus — **le cirque**	to clean — **nettoyer**	to close — **fermer**

Un clown au cirque.
A clown at the circus.

Henri nettoie sa voiture.
Henry cleans his car.

Fifi ferme la fenêtre.
Fifi closes the window.

city — **la ville**	clever — **intelligent**	closet — **l'armoire (f)**

New York est une grande ville.
New York is a big city.

Un homme intelligent apprend vite.
A clever man learns fast.

Fifi regarde dans l'armoire.
Fifi looks in the closet.

cloud **le nuage**	coffee **le café**	to comb **se peigner**

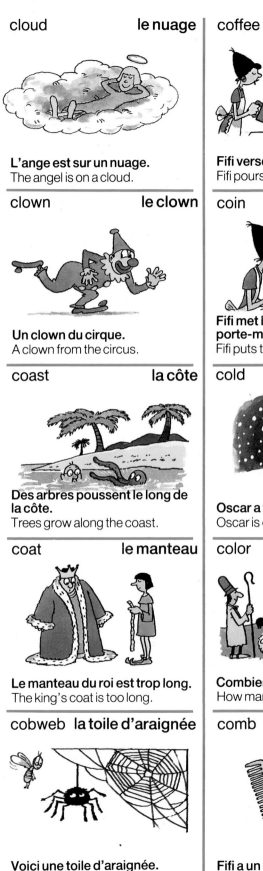

L'ange est sur un nuage.
The angel is on a cloud.

Fifi verse le café.
Fifi pours the coffee.

Fifi se peigne.
Fifi combs her hair.

clown **le clown**	coin **la pièce**	to come **venir**

Un clown du cirque.
A clown from the circus.

Fifi met les pièces* dans son porte-monnaie.
Fifi puts the coins in her purse.

Le canard vient vers Mimi.
The duck comes towards Mimi.

coast **la côte**	cold **froid**	comforter **la couette**

Des arbres poussent le long de la côte.
Trees grow along the coast.

Oscar a froid.
Oscar is cold.

Fifi a une couette rose.
Fifi has a pink comforter.

coat **le manteau**	color **la couleur**	comic strip **la bande dessinée**

Le manteau du roi est trop long.
The king's coat is too long.

Combien de couleurs* vois-tu?
How many colors do you see?

Les garçons lisent des bandes dessinées.*
The boys are reading comic strips.

cobweb **la toile d'araignée**	comb **le peigne**	computer **l'ordinateur (m)**

Voici une toile d'araignée.
Here is a cobweb.

Fifi a un grand peigne.
Fifi has a big comb.

Brains travaille sur un ordinateur.
Brains works on a computer.

conductor — **le chef d'orchestre**	to cough — **tousser**	cow — **la vache**
Herbert est chef d'orchestre. Herbert is a conductor.	**Fifi tousse.** Fifi is coughing.	**La poule est assise sur une vache.** The hen is sitting on a cow.
to cook — **faire la cuisine**	to count — **compter**	cowboy — **le cowboy**
Henri fait la cuisine. Henry is cooking.	**Mimi compte les petits gâteaux.** Mimi is counting the cupcakes.	**Le cowboy poursuit une vache.** The cowboy chases a cow.
cork — **le bouchon**	country — **le pays**	crab — **le crabe**
Le bouchon saute. The cork pops up.	**L'Angleterre est un petit pays; la Chine et l'Inde sont de grands pays.*** England is a small country; China and India are big countries.	**Le crabe court de travers.** The crab runs sideways.
corner — **le coin**	country — **la campagne**	crane — **la grue**
Ruff est au coin. Ruff is in the corner.	**Dan vit à la campagne.** Dan lives in the country.	**La grue soulève la voiture.** The crane is lifting the car.
to cost — **coûter**	to cover — **couvrir**	crayon — **le crayon de couleur**
Cette bague coûte mille francs. This ring costs 1000 francs.	**Bill se couvre la tête.** Bill covers his head.	**Mimi dessine avec des crayons* de couleur.** Mimi draws with crayons.

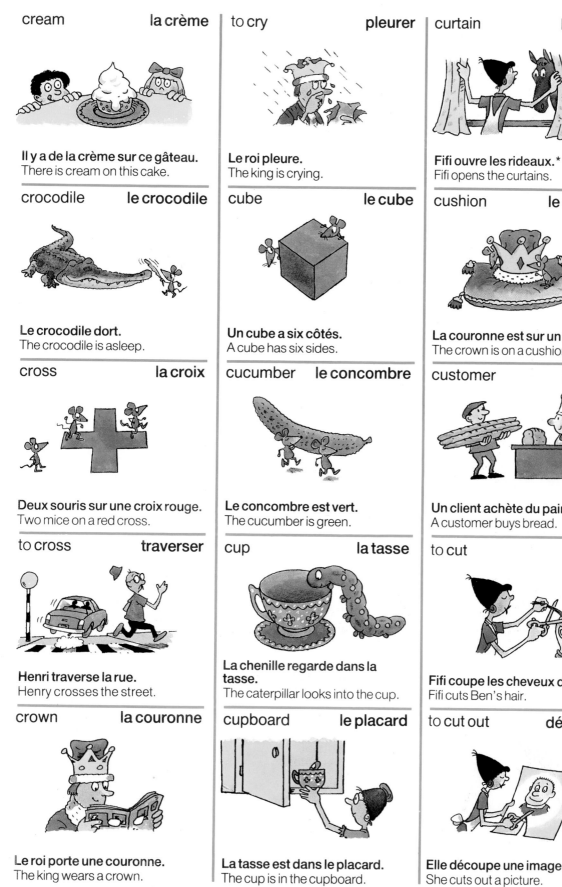

cream   **la crème**

Il y a de la crème sur ce gâteau.
There is cream on this cake.

crocodile   **le crocodile**

Le crocodile dort.
The crocodile is asleep.

cross   **la croix**

Deux souris sur une croix rouge.
Two mice on a red cross.

to cross   **traverser**

Henri traverse la rue.
Henry crosses the street.

crown   **la couronne**

Le roi porte une couronne.
The king wears a crown.

to cry   **pleurer**

Le roi pleure.
The king is crying.

cube   **le cube**

Un cube a six côtés.
A cube has six sides.

cucumber   **le concombre**

Le concombre est vert.
The cucumber is green.

cup   **la tasse**

La chenille regarde dans la tasse.
The caterpillar looks into the cup.

cupboard   **le placard**

La tasse est dans le placard.
The cup is in the cupboard.

curtain   **le rideau**

Fifi ouvre les rideaux.*
Fifi opens the curtains.

cushion   **le coussin**

La couronne est sur un coussin.
The crown is on a cushion.

customer   **le client**

Un client achète du pain.
A customer buys bread.

to cut   **couper**

Fifi coupe les cheveux de Ben.
Fifi cuts Ben's hair.

to cut out   **découper**

Elle découpe une image.
She cuts out a picture.

Dd

to dance   **danser**

Fifi danse avec Sam.
Fifi is dancing with Sam.

dancer   **la danseuse**[1]

Elle veut être danseuse.
She wants to be a dancer.

danger   **le danger**

Henri est en danger.
Henry is in danger.

to dare   **oser**

Il n'ose pas plonger.
He does not dare to dive.

---

dark   **sombre**

La pièce est sombre.
The room is dark.

daughter   **la fille**

Mimi est la fille de Mary.
Mimi is Mary's daughter.

day   **le jour**

Il y a 365 jours* dans l'année.
There are 365 days in a year.

Il y a sept jours* dans la semaine.
There are seven days in a week.

dead   **mort**

Max fait semblant d'être mort.
Max pretends to be dead.

to decide   **décider**

Bill décide d'acheter une voiture.
Bill decides to buy a car.

Décide quelle robe tu veux.
Decide which dress you want.

---

deep   **profond**

Fifi est en eau profonde.
Fifi is in deep water.

deer   **le cerf**

Max rencontre un cerf.
Max meets a deer.

dentist   **le dentiste**

Henri est chez le dentiste.
Henry is at the dentist's office.

to describe   **décrire**

Bill décrit le voleur à la police.
Bill describes the thief to the police.

Peux-tu décrire cette image?
Can you describe this picture?

desert   **le désert**

Les chameaux vivent dans le désert.
Camels live in the desert.

---

desk	le bureau	to dig	creuser	dirty	sale

desk — **le bureau**

Jake travaille à son bureau.
Jake works at his desk.

to dig — **creuser**

Max creuse un trou.
Max is digging a hole.

dirty — **sale**

Le dinosaure est sale.
The dinosaur is dirty.

diamond — **le diamant**

Fred trouve un diamant.
Fred finds a diamond.

dining room — **la salle à manger**

Les souris mangent dans la salle à manger.
The mice eat in the dining room.

dish — **le plat**

Un plat rempli de fraises.
A dish full of strawberries.

dictionary — **le dictionnaire**

Fritz a un dictionnaire.
Fritz has a dictionary.

dinner — **le dîner**

Le monstre mange son dîner.
The monster is eating his dinner.

to do — **faire**

Henri ne fait rien.
Henry is not doing anything.

to die — **mourir**

La plante est en train de mourir.
The plant is dying.

dinosaur — **le dinosaure**

Le dinosaure mange son dîner.
The dinosaur is eating his dinner.

doctor — **le médecin**[1]

Le médecin examine Sam.
The doctor examines Sam.

different — **différent**

Deux chapeaux différents.
Two different hats.

direction — **la direction**

Max change de direction.
Max changes direction.

dog — **le chien**

Le chien poursuit un lapin.
The dog chases a rabbit.

1. **Le médecin** is used both for men and women doctors.

doghouse **la niche**	dragon **le dragon**	to dress **habiller**

Ruff dort dans une niche.
Ruff sleeps in a doghouse.

Le dragon crache du feu.
The dragon breathes fire.

Fifi habille Mimi.
Fifi is dressing Mimi.

doll **la poupée**	to draw **dessiner**	to drink **boire**

Mimi joue avec sa poupée.
Mimi plays with her doll.

Fifi dessine un dragon.
Fifi is drawing a dragon.

Sam boit du lait.
Sam is drinking milk.

donkey **l'âne (m)**	drawing **le dessin**	to drive **conduire**

Henri est monté sur un âne.
Henry is riding a donkey.

Voici son dessin.
Here is her drawing.

Henri conduit sa voiture.
Henry is driving his car.

door **la porte**	to dream **rêver**	to drop **laisser tomber**

Fifi ferme la porte.
Fifi shuts the door.

Henri rêve d'araignées.
Henry dreams about spiders.

Henri laisse tomber un oeuf.
Henry drops an egg.

downstairs **en bas**	dress **la robe**	drugstore **la pharmacie**

La poupée est en bas.
The doll is downstairs.

Fifi porte une robe longue.
Fifi is wearing a long dress.

Henri est à la pharmacie.
Henry is at the drugstore.

drum   **le tambour**

Fred joue du tambour.
Fred is playing the drum.

dry   **sec, sèche**

Le sol est très sec.
The ground is very dry.

duck   **le canard**

Le canard est dans la baignoire.
The duck is in the bathtub.

dust   **la poussière**

Max se roule dans la poussière.
Max rolls in the dust.

each   **chaque**

Chaque enfant a un petit gâteau.
Each child has a cupcake.

eagle   **l'aigle (m)**

L'aigle est dans son nid.
The eagle is in its nest.

ear   **l'oreille (f)**

L'âne a de longues oreilles. *
The donkey has long ears.

early   **tôt**

Ben se lève tôt le matin.
Ben gets up early in the morning.

Je reviendrai tôt.
I will come back early.

earth   **la terre**

La Terre est ronde.
The Earth is round.

east   **l'est (m)**

L'oiseau regarde vers l'est.
The bird is facing east.

Easter   **Pâques (f. pl)**

Pâques*[1] est une fête religieuse.
Easter is a religious holiday.

Les gens ne travaillent pas le dimanche de Pâques.
People don't work on Easter Sunday.

easy   **facile**

Ce gâteau est facile à faire.
This cake is easy to make.

Les devoirs de Sam sont faciles.
Sam's homework is easy.

easy chair   **le fauteuil**

Le chat dort sur le fauteuil.
The cat is sleeping on the easy chair.

to eat   **manger**

Mimi mange du chocolat.
Mimi is eating chocolate.

edge   **le bord**

Mimi est au bord de la table.
Mimi is on the edge of the table.

egg   **l'oeuf (m)**

Mimi mange un oeuf.
Mimi is eating an egg.

elbow   **le coude**

Henri se cogne le coude.
Henry hits his elbow.

elephant   **l'éléphant (m)**

Un éléphant a de grandes oreilles.
An elephant has big ears.

elevator   **l'ascenseur (m)**

Henri entre dans l'ascenseur.
Henry enters the elevator.

empty   **vide**

Le sac est vide.
The bag is empty.

to empty   **vider**

Henri vide le seau.
Henry empties the bucket.

end   **le bout**

La souris se balance au bout de la corde.
The mouse is swinging at the end of the rope.

enough   **assez**

Fifi a assez d'argent pour acheter une nouvelle voiture.
Fifi has enough money to buy a new car.

As-tu assez mangé?
Have you had enough to eat?

to enter   **entrer**

Le roi entre dans la pièce.
The king enters the room.

entrance   **l'entrée (f)**

L'entrée d'une caverne.
The entrance to a cave.

envelope   **l'enveloppe (f)**

Fifi ouvre l'enveloppe.
Fifi opens the envelope.

to escape   **s'évader**

Le prisonnier s'évade.
The prisoner escapes.

evening   **le soir**

Le soleil se couche le soir.
The sun sets in the evening.

every   **tous, toutes**

Tous les cochons sont roses.
Every pig is pink.

everyone   **tout le monde**

Tout le monde porte un chapeau.
Everyone is wearing a hat.

everything   **tout**

Tout est vert.
Everything is green.

everywhere   **partout**

Fifi cherche son chat partout.
Fifi looks everywhere for her cat.

Mon chien me suit partout.
My dog follows me everywhere.

except   **sauf**

Tous les cochons sont roses sauf un.
Every pig is pink except one.

exciting   **passionnant**

Jake lit un livre passionnant.
Jake reads an exciting book.

experiment   **l'expérience**

Brains fait une expérience.
Brains does an experiment.

to explain   **expliquer**

Fifi explique pourquoi elle veut une voiture.
Fifi explains why she wants a car.

Explique-moi comment cela marche.
Explain to me how this works.

eyes   **les yeux**[1]

Le chat a les yeux* bleus.
The cat has blue eyes.

face   **la figure**

Fifi se lave la figure.
Fifi washes her face.

factory   **l'usine (f)**

Bill travaille dans une usine.
Bill works in a factory.

fairy   **la fée**

La fée est assise sur une fleur.
The fairy sits on a flower

to fall   **tomber**

La fée tombe.
The fairy falls off.

family   **la famille**

La famille de Fifi.
Fifi's family.

famous   **célèbre**

Will est un peintre célèbre.
Will is a famous painter.

1. eye (singular): **l'oeil (m)**

far   **loin**

La maison est loin.
The house is far away.

farm   **la ferme**

La ferme est à la campagne.
The farm is in the country.

farmer   **le fermier**

Le fermier habite une ferme.
The farmer lives on a farm.

fast   **vite**

Le fermier court vite.
The farmer runs fast.

fat   **gros, grosse**

Cette fée est grosse.
This fairy is fat.

father   **le père**

Mimi est avec son père.
Mimi is with her father.

faucet   **le robinet**

La souris ouvre le robinet.
The mouse turns on the faucet.

feather   **la plume**

Un oiseau à plumes* jaunes.
A bird with yellow feathers.

to feed   **nourrir**

Mimi nourrit les canards.
Mimi feeds the ducks.

to feel   **toucher**

Bill touche la chaise.
Bill feels the chair.

feet   **les pieds (m. pl)**

Voici deux grands pieds.*
Here are two big feet.

fence   **la clôture**

La vache saute par-dessus la clôture.
The cow jumps over the fence.

few   **peu**

Cet oiseau a peu de plumes.
This bird has few feathers.

field   **le champ**

Les vaches sont dans un champ.
The cows are in a field.

to fight   **se battre**

Bill et Ben se battent.
Bill and Ben are fighting.

to fill	remplir

Fifi remplit le verre.
Fifi fills the glass.

to find	trouver

Bill trouve son livre.
Bill finds his book.

finger	le doigt

Quatre doigts* et un pouce.
Four fingers and a thumb.

to finish	finir

Fifi finit son dîner.
Fifi finishes her dinner.

fire	le feu

Ces hommes sont assis près du feu.
These men sit by the fire.

fireman	le pompier

Les pompiers* éteignent le feu.
The firemen put out the fire.

fireworks	le feu d'artifice[1]

Un feu d'artifice dans le ciel.
Fireworks in the sky.

first	premier, première

Bill est le premier de la file.
Bill is first in line.

fish	le poisson

Un gros poisson et un petit poisson.
A big fish and a little fish.

to fish	pêcher à la ligne

Jean pêche à la ligne.
John is fishing.

to fix	réparer

Ben répare sa bicyclette.
Ben is fixing his bicycle.

flag	le drapeau

Henri porte un drapeau.
Henry is carrying a flag.

flame	la flamme

Mimi souffle la flamme.
Mimi blows out the flame.

flat	plat

Cette maison a un toit plat.
This house has a flat roof.

floor	le plancher

Ruff est couché sur le plancher.
Ruff is lying on the floor.

1. The word for 'fireworks' is always singular in French.

flour — la farine

Bill tamise la farine.
Bill is sifting the flour.

to flow — couler

La rivière coule vers la mer.
The river flows towards the sea.

flower — la fleur

Henri donne une fleur à Fifi.
Henry gives Fifi a flower.

fly — la mouche

Il y a une mouche sur la fleur.
There is a fly on the flower.

to fly — voler

La mouche vole.
The fly is flying.

fog — le brouillard

Henri est perdu dans le brouillard.
Henry is lost in the fog.

to follow — suivre

Henri suit un chien.
Henry is following a dog.

food — la nourriture

Une assiette pleine de nourriture.
A plate full of food.

for — pour

Ce cadeau est pour Ben.
This present is for Ben.

forehead — le front

Henri se cogne le front.
Henry hits his forehead.

forest — la forêt

Il y a beaucoup d'arbres dans une forêt.
There are many trees in a forest.

to forget — oublier

Bill a oublié mon nom.
Bill has forgotten my name.

Ne m'oubliez pas!
Don't forget me!

J'ai oublié où il habite.
I have forgotten where he lives.

fork — la fourchette

Ben tient une fourchette.
Ben is holding a fork.

fox — le renard

Le renard est roux.
The fox is red.

to freeze — geler

Quand l'eau gèle, elle se transforme en glace.
When water freezes it turns into ice.

congeler

Fifi congèle les aliments au congélateur.
Fifi freezes food in the freezer.

French fries   les frites (f. pl)

Ben a une assiette de frites. *
Ben has a plate of French fries.

friend   l'ami (m) [1]

Sam et Fifi sont amis. *
Sam and Fifi are friends.

to frighten   faire peur à

Fifi fait peur à son ami.
Fifi frightens her friend.

frog   la grenouille

La grenouille saute.
The frog is jumping.

from   de

Cette lettre vient de France.
This letter is from France.

Elle est de Pierre à Fifi.
It is from Pierre to Fifi.

Je vais au cinéma de temps en temps.
I go to the movies from time to time.

in front of   devant

Ben est devant Bill.
Ben is in front of Bill.

frost   le givre

Il y a du givre sur la vitre.
There is frost on the window.

fruit   le fruit

Plusieurs sortes de fruits. *
Several kinds of fruit.

fry   faire cuire

Ben fait cuire un oeuf sur le plat.
Ben fries an egg.

frying pan   la poêle

Des oeufs en train de cuire dans une poêle.
Eggs frying in a frying pan.

full   plein

La baignoire est pleine d'eau.
The bathtub is full of water.

funny   drôle

Le clown est drôle.
The clown is funny.

fur   la fourrure

Le lapin a une fourrure blanche.
The rabbit has white fur.

game   le jeu

Un jeu de colin-maillard.
A game of blindman's buff.

| garage | **le garage** | gate | **la barrière** | girl | **la fille** |

La voiture est dans le garage.
The car is in the garage.

Le fermier ferme la barrière.
The farmer shuts the gate.

La petite fille poursuit le chat.
The little girl chases the cat.

| garbage can | **la poubelle** | to get up | **se lever** | to give | **donner** |

Bill regarde dans la poubelle.
Bill looks in the garbage can.

Ben se lève à sept heures.
Ben gets up at 7 o'clock.

L'enfant donne une fleur à Ben.
The child gives Ben a flower.

| garden | **le jardin** | ghost | **le fantôme** | glass | **le verre** |

Des fleurs poussent dans le jardin.
Flowers grow in the garden.

Le fantôme fait peur à Henri.
The ghost frightens Henry.

Le verre est plein de lait.
The glass is full of milk.

| gas | **le gaz** | giant | **le géant** | glasses | **les lunettes (f. pl)** |

Henri allume la cuisinière à gaz.
Henry lights the gas stove.

Le géant est un homme très grand.
The giant is a very big man.

Henri porte des lunettes.*
Henry is wearing glasses.

| gasoline | **l'essence (f)** | giraffe | **la girafe** | glove | **le gant** |

Henri met de l'essence dans sa voiture.
Henry puts gasoline in his car.

La girafe mange des feuilles.
The giraffe is eating leaves.

Une paire de gants* rouges.
A pair of red gloves.

32

to go	aller	grape	le raisin	grocer	l'épicier (m)

Les enfants vont en classe.
The children go to school.

Voici une grappe de raisin.
Here is a bunch of grapes.

L'épicier vend du fromage.
The grocer is selling cheese.

goat	la chèvre	grapefruit	le pample-mousse	ground	le sol

La chèvre mord Henri.
The goat bites Henry.

Fifi mange un pamplemousse.
Fifi eats grapefruit.

Mimi est assise sur le sol.
Mimi is sitting on the ground.

gold	l'or (m)	grass	l'herbe (f)	group	le groupe

Fifi a une chaîne d'or.
Fifi has a gold chain.

Ruff se roule dans l'herbe.
Ruff is rolling in the grass.

Voici un groupe de garçons.
Here is a group of boys.

good	bon, bonne	gray	gris	to grow	grandir

Ben est un bon boulanger.
Ben is a good baker.

Le gros chat est gris.
The big cat is gray.

Mimi grandit.
Mimi is growing.

goose	l'oie (f)	green	vert	guest	l'invité (m)

L'oie poursuit la chèvre.
The goose chases the goat.

L'herbe est verte.
The grass is green.

Fifi accueille son invité.
Fifi welcomes her guest.

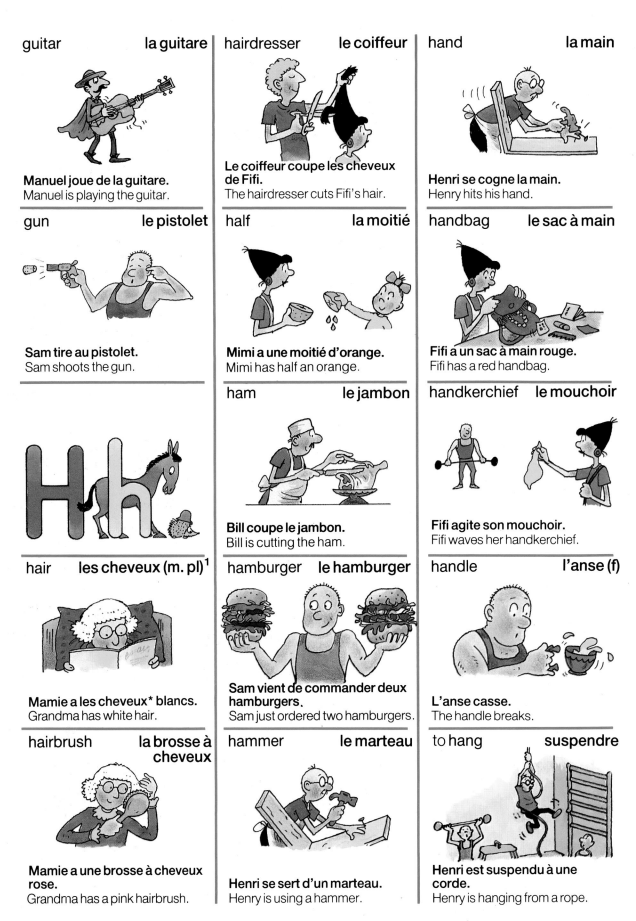

guitar **la guitare**

Manuel joue de la guitare.
Manuel is playing the guitar.

hairdresser **le coiffeur**

Le coiffeur coupe les cheveux de Fifi.
The hairdresser cuts Fifi's hair.

hand **la main**

Henri se cogne la main.
Henry hits his hand.

gun **le pistolet**

Sam tire au pistolet.
Sam shoots the gun.

half **la moitié**

Mimi a une moitié d'orange.
Mimi has half an orange.

handbag **le sac à main**

Fifi a un sac à main rouge.
Fifi has a red handbag.

ham **le jambon**

Bill coupe le jambon.
Bill is cutting the ham.

handkerchief **le mouchoir**

Fifi agite son mouchoir.
Fifi waves her handkerchief.

hair **les cheveux (m. pl)[1]**

Mamie a les cheveux* blancs.
Grandma has white hair.

hamburger **le hamburger**

Sam vient de commander deux hamburgers.
Sam just ordered two hamburgers.

handle **l'anse (f)**

L'anse casse.
The handle breaks.

hairbrush **la brosse à cheveux**

Mamie a une brosse à cheveux rose.
Grandma has a pink hairbrush.

hammer **le marteau**

Henri se sert d'un marteau.
Henry is using a hammer.

to hang **suspendre**

Henri est suspendu à une corde.
Henry is hanging from a rope.

34   1. The word for 'hair' is always plural in French.

to happen	se passer

Que se passe-t-il?
What is happening?

	arriver

Quand l'accident est-il arrivé?
When did the accident happen?

Comment cela est-il arrivé?
How did it happen?

to have	avoir[1]

Bill et Ben ont deux chats.
Bill and Ben have two cats.

heart	le coeur

Quand tu cours, ton coeur bat plus vite.
When you run, your heart beats faster.

Je t'aime de tout mon coeur.
I love you with all my heart.

Je connais cette chanson par coeur.
I know this song by heart.

happy	content

Bill est content de voir Ben.
Bill is happy to see Ben.

hay	le foin

Georges coupe l'herbe pour faire du foin.
George cuts grass to make hay.

heavy	lourd

Cette pierre est lourde.
This rock is heavy.

harbor	le port

Les bateaux sont dans le port.
The boats are in the harbor.

head	la tête

Henri a un oiseau sur la tête.
Henry has a bird on his head.

hedge	la haie

Henri taille la haie.
Henry is cutting the hedge.

hard	dur

Ce matelas est dur.
This mattress is hard.

headlights	les phares (f. pl)

Les phares* éclairent.
The headlights are shining.

helicopter	l'hélicoptère (m)

L'hélicoptère vole.
The helicopter is flying.

hat	le chapeau

Fifi porte un joli chapeau.
Fifi is wearing a pretty hat.

to hear	entendre

Papy n'entend pas bien.
Grandpa cannot hear well.

to help	aider

Bill aide Ben.
Bill is helping Ben.

1. See page 83.

hen   **la poule**

La poule mange des graines.
The hen is eating seeds.

here   **ici**

Je reste ici.
I am staying here.

Viens ici.
Come here.

here is   **voici**

Voici notre maison.
Here is our house.

to hide   **se cacher**

Le voleur se cache.
The thief is hiding.

high   **haut**

Voici une haute montagne.
This is a high mountain.

high   **haut**

L'oiseau vole haut dans le ciel.
The bird flies high in the sky.

hill   **la colline**

La maison est sur une colline.
The house is on a hill.

hippopotamus   **l'hippopotame (m)**

Un hippopotame couvert de boue.
A hippopotamus covered with mud.

to hit   **frapper**

Mimi frappe Ruff.
Mimi hits Ruff.

to hold   **tenir**

La sorcière tient son balai.
The witch is holding her broom.

hole   **le trou**

Ruff creuse un trou.
Ruff is digging a hole.

homework   **les devoirs (m. pl)[1]**

**Tim fait ses devoirs.*
Tim is doing his homework.

honey   **le miel**

Le miel est dans le pot.
The honey is in the jar.

hook   **le crochet**

Le chapeau est suspendu à un crochet.
The hat is hanging on a hook.

to hop   **sauter**

Le lapin saute par-dessus Ruff.
The rabbit hops over Ruff.

horse   **le cheval**

Henri monte à cheval.
Henry is riding a horse.

| hospital   l'hôpital (m) | house   la maison | husband   le mari |

Henri est à l'hôpital.
Henry is in the hospital.

Fritz habite dans une grande maison.
Fritz lives in a big house.

Fritz est le mari de Heidi.
Fritz is Heidi's husband.

hot   **chaud**

how   **comment**

Comment vas-tu?
How are you?

Comment fait-on un gâteau?
How do you make a cake?

Comment dit-on cela en français?
How do you say it in French?

La soupe est chaude.
The soup is hot.

hot dog   **le hot-dog**

to be hungry   **avoir faim**

ice   **la glace**

Fifi mange un hot-dog.
Fifi is eating a hot dog.

Mimi a faim.
Mimi is hungry.

La mare est couverte de glace.
The pond is covered with ice.

hotel   **l'hôtel (m)**

to hurry   **se dépêcher**

ice cream   **la glace**

Fifi va à l'hôtel.
Fifi is going to a hotel.

Henri se dépêche.
Henry is hurrying.

Mimi mange une glace.
Mimi is eating ice cream.

hour   **l'heure (f)**

to hurt   **blesser, se blesser**[1]

idea   **l'idée (f)**

Il y a 24 heures* dans une journée.
There are 24 hours in a day.

Il y a 60 minutes dans une heure.
There are 60 minutes in an hour.

Henri s'est blessé le pied avec une pierre.
Henry hurt his foot with a rock.

Quelle bonne idée!
What a good idea!

Je viens d'avoir une idée.
I have just had an idea.

Je n'ai pas la moindre idée.
I do not have the slightest idea.

1. **blesser:** to hurt (someone else), **se blesser:** to hurt oneself or a part of oneself.

if	**si**	**instead of**	**au lieu de**	**island**	**l'île (f)**

if — **si**

Viens si tu peux.
Come if you can.

Fifi demande si Sam est à la maison.
Fifi asks if Sam is at home.

Il t'aidera si tu le demandes.
He will help you if you ask him.

instead of — **au lieu de**

Fifi mange du miel au lieu de manger du sucre.
Fifi eats honey instead of sugar.

Il joue au lieu de travailler.
He is playing instead of working.

island — **l'île (f)**

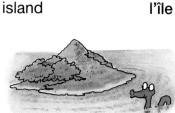

Une île dans la mer.
An island in the sea.

ill — **malade**

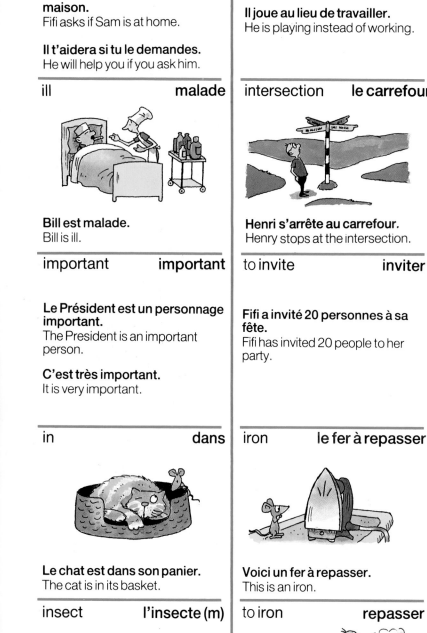

Bill est malade.
Bill is ill.

intersection — **le carrefour**

Henri s'arrête au carrefour.
Henry stops at the intersection.

j — **J**

important — **important**

Le Président est un personnage important.
The President is an important person.

C'est très important.
It is very important.

to invite — **inviter**

Fifi a invité 20 personnes à sa fête.
Fifi has invited 20 people to her party.

jacket — **la veste**

Fritz a une veste verte.
Fritz has a green jacket.

in — **dans**

Le chat est dans son panier.
The cat is in its basket.

iron — **le fer à repasser**

Voici un fer à repasser.
This is an iron.

jam — **la confiture**

Un pot de confiture de fraises.
A jar of strawberry jam.

insect — **l'insecte (m)**

Voici des insectes.*
These are insects.

to iron — **repasser**

Henri repasse sa chemise.
Henry is ironing his shirt.

jar — **le bocal**

Voici un bocal vide.
This is an empty jar.

jeans **le blue-jean**

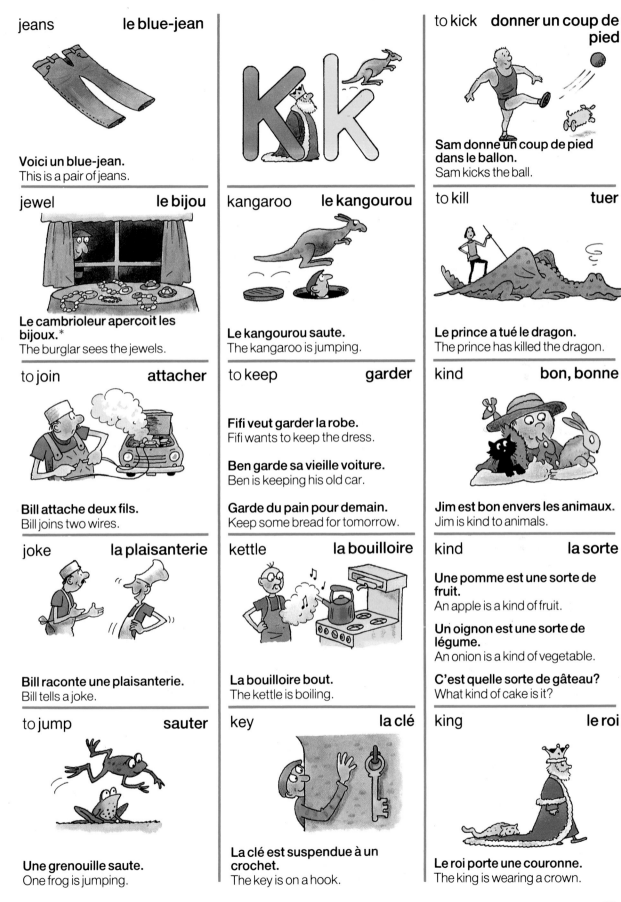

Voici un blue-jean.
This is a pair of jeans.

jewel **le bijou**

Le cambrioleur apercoit les bijoux.*
The burglar sees the jewels.

to join **attacher**

Bill attache deux fils.
Bill joins two wires.

joke **la plaisanterie**

Bill raconte une plaisanterie.
Bill tells a joke.

to jump **sauter**

Une grenouille saute.
One frog is jumping.

K k

kangaroo **le kangourou**

Le kangourou saute.
The kangaroo is jumping.

to keep **garder**

Fifi veut garder la robe.
Fifi wants to keep the dress.

Ben garde sa vieille voiture.
Ben is keeping his old car.

Garde du pain pour demain.
Keep some bread for tomorrow.

kettle **la bouilloire**

La bouilloire bout.
The kettle is boiling.

key **la clé**

La clé est suspendue à un crochet.
The key is on a hook.

to kick **donner un coup de pied**

Sam donne un coup de pied dans le ballon.
Sam kicks the ball.

to kill **tuer**

Le prince a tué le dragon.
The prince has killed the dragon.

kind **bon, bonne**

Jim est bon envers les animaux.
Jim is kind to animals.

kind **la sorte**

Une pomme est une sorte de fruit.
An apple is a kind of fruit.

Un oignon est une sorte de légume.
An onion is a kind of vegetable.

C'est quelle sorte de gâteau?
What kind of cake is it?

king **le roi**

Le roi porte une couronne.
The king is wearing a crown.

to kiss **embrasser**	knee **le genou**	knot **le noeud**

Fifi embrasse Sam.
Fifi is kissing Sam.

Henri tombe sur le genou.
Henry falls on his knee.

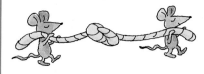

Il y a un noeud dans la ficelle.
The string has a knot in it.

kitchen **la cuisine**	knife **le couteau**	to know **savoir**[1]

Fritz sait nager.
Fritz knows how to swim.

Je sais que deux et deux font quatre.
I know that two and two are four.

Ben est dans la cuisine.
Ben is in the kitchen.

Bill coupe du pain avec un couteau.
Bill cuts bread with a knife.

connaître[2]

Sam connaît Ben.
Sam knows Ben.

kite **le cerf-volant**	to knit **tricoter**	

Bill joue avec un cerf-volant.
Bill is playing with a kite.

Henri tricote.
Henry is knitting.

kitten **le chaton**	knitting **le tricot**	lace **la dentelle**

Un chaton est un bébé chat.
A kitten is a baby cat.

Voici son tricot.
This is his knitting.

Cette robe est en dentelle.
This dress is made of lace.

knapsack **le cartable**	to knock **frapper**	ladder **l'échelle (f)**

Terry a un cartable rouge.
Terry has a red knapsack.

Sam frappe à la porte.
Sam knocks on the door.

Henri monte à l'échelle.
Henry climbs the ladder.

lake   **le lac**

Il y a des bateaux sur le lac.
There are boats on the lake.

lamb   **l'agneau (m)**

Un agneau est un bébé mouton.
A lamb is a baby sheep.

lamp   **la lampe**

Fifi lit à la lumière de la lampe.
Fifi is reading by the lamp.

last   **dernier, dernière**

Bill est le dernier de la file.
Ben is the last in line.

to last   **durer**

Le film dure une heure.
The movie lasts an hour.

Le beau temps a duré cinq jours.
The good weather lasted for five days.

Combien de temps cela va-t-il durer?
How long will it last?

late   **en retard**

Tim est en retard.
Tim is late.

       tard

Il se couche tard.
He goes to bed late.

Est-ce trop tard pour le film?
Am I too late for the movie?

to laugh   **rire**

Ben rit.
Ben is laughing.

lawn   **le gazon**

Fifi tond le gazon.
Fifi is mowing the lawn.

lazy   **paresseux**

Marc est paresseux.
Mark is lazy.

to lead   **guider**

Ben guide les enfants.
Ben is leading the children.

leaf   **la feuille**

La fourmi transporte une feuille.
The ant is carrying a leaf.

to leak   **fuir**

Le robinet de Ben fuit.
Ben's faucet is leaking.

to lean   **s'appuyer**

Bruno s'appuie contre la clôture.
Bruno is leaning on the fence.

to learn   **apprendre**

Fifi apprend à conduire.
Fifi is learning how to drive.

J'apprends le français à l'école.
I am learning French at school.

leash   **la laisse**

Le chien est en laisse.
The dog is on a leash.

leather — **le cuir**

Ce sac est en cuir.
This purse is made of leather.

to leave — **quitter**

Fifi quitte la maison.
Fifi is leaving the house.

left — **gauche**

Fritz tourne à gauche.
Fritz turns left.

leg — **la jambe**

Henri patine sur une jambe.
Henry is skating on one leg.

lemon — **le citron**

Fifi coupe un citron en deux.
Fifi cuts a lemon in half.

lesson — **la leçon**

Les élèves ont une leçon.
The students are having a lesson.

letter — **la lettre**

Sam lit une lettre.
Sam is reading a letter.

lettuce — **la laitue**

La chenille aime la laitue.
The caterpillar likes lettuce.

library — **la bibliothèque**

Bill est dans la bibliothèque.
Bill is in the library.

to lick — **lécher**

Mimi lèche sa glace.
Mimi licks her ice cream.

lid — **le couvercle**

Bill met le couvercle sur le bocal.
Bill puts the lid on the jar.

life — **la vie**

Les papillons ont la vie courte.
Butterflies have a short life.

La vie est très tranquille ici.
Life is very quiet here.

Il m'a sauvé la vie.
He saved my life.

to lift — **soulever**

La grue soulève une voiture.
The crane is lifting a car.

light — **léger, légère**

La danseuse est légère.
The dancer is light.

light — **la lumière**

La lumière est allumée.
The light is on.

to light **allumer**	**lip** **la lèvre**	**long** **long, longue**
Fritz allume une allumette. Fritz lights a match.	**Il a de grosses lèvres* rouges.** He has big red lips.	**Le serpent est long.** The snake is long.
lighthouse **le phare**	**list** **la liste**	**to look at** **regarder**
Le phare est sur la côte. The lighthouse is on the coast.	**Henri fait une longue liste.** Henry makes a long list.	**Fifi regarde un tableau.** Fifi is looking at a picture.
lightning **l'éclair (m)**	**to listen** **écouter**	**to look for** **chercher**
L'éclair illumine le ciel. Lightning lights up the sky.	**Papy écoute la radio.** Grandpa listens to the radio.	**Henri cherche un livre.** Henry is looking for a book.
to like **aimer bien**	**to live** **vivre**	**(to be) lost** **s'égarer**
Fifi aime bien Ben. Fifi likes Ben.	**Rob vit sur une île.** Rob lives on an island.	**Henri s'est égaré.** Henry is lost.
lion **le lion**	**living room** **le salon**	**a lot of** **beaucoup de**
Le lion rugit. The lion is roaring.	**Voici un salon.** This is a living room.	**Il y a beaucoup d'oiseaux dans l'arbre.** There are a lot of birds in the tree.

loud	**bruyant**

La fanfare est bruyante.
The band is loud.

to love	**aimer**

Sam aime Fifi.
Sam loves Fifi.

low	**bas, basse**

Le mur est bas.
The wall is low.

to have lunch	**déjeuner**

Mimi déjeune à midi.
Mimi has lunch at noon.

M m

machine	**la machine**

Toutes ces machines* marchent.
All these machines work.

magazine	**la revue**

Henri lit une revue.
Henry is reading a magazine.

magician	**le prestidigitateur**

Voici un prestidigitateur.
Here is a magician.

mailman	**le facteur**

Le facteur apporte des lettres.
The mailman brings letters.

to make	**faire**

Ben fait un gâteau.
Ben is making a cake.

man	**l'homme (m)**

Un homme et deux femmes.
One man and two women.

many	**beaucoup de**

Beaucoup de revues à vendre.
Many magazines for sale.

map	**la carte**

Henri regarde une carte.
Henry looks at a map.

mark	**la tache**

Il y a une tache sur la carte.
There is a mark on the map.

market	**le marché**

Voici un marché en plein air.
This is an open-air market.

to marry — épouser

Sam épouse Fifi.
Sam is marrying Fifi.

mask — le masque

Qui porte le masque?
Who is wearing the mask?

match — l'allumette (f)

Fred allume une allumette.
Fred lights a match.

to measure — mesurer

Fifi mesure Mimi.
Fifi measures Mimi.

meat — la viande

Le boucher coupe de la viande.
The butcher is chopping meat.

medicine — le médicament

L'infirmière donne un médicament à Mimi.
The nurse gives Mimi medicine.

to meet — rencontrer

Bill rencontre Ben.
Bill meets Ben.

to melt — fondre

La glace fond.
The ice cream is melting.

menu — le menu

Fifi lit le menu.
Fifi reads the menu.

metal — le métal

Une voiture est faite de métal.
A car is made of metal.

middle — le milieu

Le cochon est au milieu des chèvres.
The pig is in the middle of the goats.

milk — le lait

Mimi boit du lait.
Mimi is drinking milk.

minute — la minute

Il y a 60 secondes dans une minute.
There are 60 seconds in a minute.

Il y a 60 minutes* dans une heure.
There are 60 minutes in an hour.

mirror — la glace

Le chat regarde dans la glace.
The cat looks in the mirror.

to miss — rater

Henri a raté l'autobus.
Henry has missed the bus.

| model | **le modèle réduit** | moon | **la lune** | motorcycle | **la moto** |

model — **le modèle réduit**

Fritz fait un modèle réduit d'avion.
Fritz is making a model airplane.

moon — **la lune**

La lune est dans le ciel.
The moon is in the sky.

motorcycle — **la moto**

Henri conduit une moto.
Henry is riding a motorcycle.

money — **l'argent (m)**

Ben compte son argent.
Ben is counting his money.

more — **plus**

Bill a plus d'argent que Ben.
Bill has more money than Ben.

mountain — **la montagne**

Voici une haute montagne.
This is a high mountain.

monkey — **le singe**

Le singe se balance.
The monkey is swinging.

morning — **le matin**

Avant midi, c'est le matin.
Morning comes before noon.

Nous nous levons le matin.
We get up in the morning.

Le matin, les gens vont au travail et les enfants à l'école.
In the morning people go to work and children go to school.

mouse — **la souris**

Une des souris* est rose.
One of the mice is pink.

monster — **le monstre**

Le monstre est aimable.
The monster is friendly.

most — **la plupart**

La plupart des pommes sont rouges.
Most of the apples are red.

mouth — **la bouche**

Cet homme a une grande bouche.
This man has a big mouth.

month — **le mois**

Il y a douze mois* dans l'année.
There are twelve months in a year.

Janvier est le premier mois de l'année.
January is the first month of the year.

Décembre est le dernier mois.
December is the last month.

mother — **la mère**

Mary est la mère de Mimi.
Mary is Mimi's mother.

to move — **déplacer**

Ils déplacent la table.
They are moving the table.

46

movie	le film	music	la musique	naughty	vilain

Fifi et Sam regardent un film.
Fifi and Sam watch a movie.

La fanfare joue de la musique.
The band plays music.

Mimi est vilaine.
Mimi is naughty.

movie theater	le cinéma	mustache	la moustache	near	près de

Fifi est au cinéma.
Fifi is at the movie theater.

Cet homme a une moustache.
This man has a mustache.

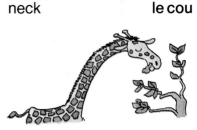

L'arbre est près de la maison.
The tree is near the house.

much	beaucoup

As-tu beaucoup d'argent?
Do you have much money?

Je me sens beaucoup mieux.
I feel much better.

A-t-il eu beaucoup de succès?
Has he had much success?

neck	le cou

Une girafe a un long cou.
A giraffe has a long neck.

mud	la boue	nail	le clou	necklace	le collier

Le monstre joue dans la boue.
The monster is playing in the mud.

Henri tape sur un clou.
Henry hits a nail.

Fifi porte un collier.
Fifi is wearing a necklace.

mushroom	le champignon	name	le nom	to need	avoir besoin de

Une souris sur un champignon.
A mouse on a mushroom.

Mimi écrit son nom.
Mimi writes her name.

Mimi a besoin d'un bain.
Mimi needs a bath.

needle	l'aiguille (f)	next to	à côté de	nose	le nez

Fifi enfile une aiguille.
Fifi threads a needle.

Fifi est assise à côté de Sam.
Fifi is sitting next to Sam.

Henri a le nez rouge.
Henry has a red nose.

nest	le nid	night	la nuit	notebook	le carnet

Les oisillons vivent dans un nid.
Baby birds live in a nest.

Il fait nuit.
It is night.

L'homme consulte son carnet.
The man looks at his notebook.

never	ne . . . jamais	nobody	ne . . . personne	nothing	rien

Fifi ne mange jamais de fromage.
Fifi never eats cheese.

Je ne regarde jamais la télévision.
I never watch television.

Papy ne sort jamais.
Grandpa never goes out.

Personne ne porte de chapeau.
Nobody is wearing a hat.

Il n'y a rien dans la boîte.
There is nothing in the box.

new	nouveau, nouvelle	noise	le bruit	now	maintenant

Il est maintenant cinq heures.
It is now 5 o'clock.

Je dois partir maintenant.
I must go now.

Maintenant je rentre à la maison.
Now I am going home.

Ben a une nouvelle voiture.
Ben has a new car.

Mimi fait du bruit.
Mimi is making noise.

newspaper	le journal	north	le nord	number	le chiffre

Bill lit le journal.
Bill reads the newspaper.

L'oiseau regarde vers le nord.
The bird is facing north.

Voici des chiffres.*
Here are some numbers.

nurse	l'infirmière (f)

Une infirmière donne un médicament à Ben.
A nurse gives Ben medicine.

nut	la noix

Mimi mange des noix.
Mimi is eating nuts.

octopus	la pieuvre

Voici une pieuvre.
Here is an octopus.

to offer	offrir

Sam offre des fleurs à Fifi.
Sam offers Fifi flowers.

office	le bureau

Jake travaille dans un bureau.
Jake works in an office.

often	souvent

Le téléphone sonne souvent.
The telephone often rings.

to oil	huiler

Tim huile sa bicyclette.
Tim oils his bicycle.

old	vieux, vieille

Papy est un vieux monsieur.
Grandpa is an old man.

on	sur

La tasse est sur la table.
The cup is on the table.

onion	l'oignon (m)

Henri coupe un oignon.
Henry is slicing an onion.

only	seulement

Un cochon seulement est noir.
Only one pig is black.

to open	ouvrir

Fifi ouvre la porte.
Fifi opens the door.

open	ouvert

Le magasin est ouvert.
The store is open.

opposite	le contraire

Chaud est le contraire de froid.
Hot is the opposite of cold.

or	ou

Quelles chaussures veux-tu, les bleues ou les rouges?
Which shoes do you want, the blue ones or the red ones?

Tu peux avoir l'une ou l'autre paire.
You can have one pair or the other.

orange	orange

Henri a des chaussettes orange.
Henry has orange socks.

orange	l'orange (f)

Une orange est orange.
An orange is orange.

to order	commander

Fritz commande son dîner.
Fritz orders his dinner.

other	autre

Où est l'autre chaussette?
Where is the other sock?

---

out of	hors de

Les jouets sont hors de la boîte.
The toys are out of the box.

outside	dehors

Mimi joue dehors.
Mimi is playing outside.

over	par-dessus

Le cochon saute par-dessus la clôture.
The pig jumps over the fence.

owl	le hibou

Le hibou est dans l'arbre.
The owl is in the tree.

P p

---

package	le paquet

Le facteur apporte un paquet.
The mailman brings a package.

page	la page

Voici la première page.
This is the first page.

to paint	peindre

L'artiste peint.
The artist is painting.

paints	les couleurs (f. pl)

Voici ses couleurs.*
These are her paints.

pair	la paire

Une paire de chaussettes orange.
A pair of orange socks.

palace **le palais**	parents **les parents (m. pl)**	to pass **passer devant**
Le roi vit dans un palais. The king lives in a palace.	**Mimi est avec ses parents.** * Mimi is with her parents.	**Henri passe devant Bruno.** Henry passes in front of Bruno.
pancake **la crêpe**	park **le parc**	passport **le passeport**
Bill fait des crêpes. * Bill is making pancakes.	**Fifi se promène dans le parc.** Fifi is walking in the park.	**Ben montre son passeport.** Ben shows his passport.
pants **le pantalon**[1]	to park **garer**	path **le chemin**
Ben porte un pantalon rouge. Ben is wearing red pants.	**Henri gare sa voiture.** Henry is parking his car.	**Le chemin traverse le champ.** The path crosses the field.
paper **le papier**	parrot **le perroquet**	patient **le malade**
Mimi peint sur du papier. Mimi is painting on paper.	**Le perroquet rit.** The parrot is laughing.	**Le malade est au lit.** The patient is in bed.
parachute **le parachute**	party **la surprise-partie**	paw **la patte**
Le parachute descend. The parachute is coming down.	**C'est la surprise-partie de Fifi.** It is Fifi's party.	**Le chat se lèche la patte.** The cat is licking its paw.

1. This word is used in the singular.

to pay	**payer**

Fifi paie le boulanger.
Fifi pays the baker.

pea	**le petit pois**[1]

Mimi mange des petits pois.*
Mimi is eating peas.

peach	**la pêche**

Bill mange une pêche.
Bill is eating a peach.

pear	**la poire**

Ben mange une poire.
Ben is eating a pear.

pen	**le stylo**

Fifi écrit avec un stylo.
Fifi writes with a pen.

---

pencil	**le crayon**

Elle dessine avec un crayon.
She draws with a pencil.

people	**les gens (m. pl)**

Ces gens* parlent.
These people are talking.

pepper	**le poivre**

Bill met du poivre dans son assiette.
Bill puts pepper on his plate.

perhaps	**peut-être**

Il va peut-être pleuvoir.
Perhaps it will rain.

Il s'est peut-être perdu.
Perhaps he is lost.

photograph	**la photo**

Voici une photo de Fifi.
This is a photograph of Fifi.

---

piano	**le piano**

Fritz joue du piano.
Fritz plays the piano.

to pick	**cueillir**

Les gens cueillent des poires.
The people are picking pears.

to pick up	**ramasser**

Fifi ramasse une poire.
Fifi picks up a pear.

picnic	**le pique-nique**

Les amis font un pique-nique.
The friends are having a picnic.

picture	**le tableau**

Un tableau représentant un pique-nique.
A picture of a picnic.

1. This word is only used in the plural.

pie **la tourte**	pilot **le pilote**	pipe **la pipe**

Bill coupe la tourte.
Bill cuts the pie.

piece   le morceau

Mimi mange un morceau de tourte.
Mimi eats a piece of pie.

pig   le cochon

Voici un cochon rose.
This is a pink pig.

pile   la pile

Henri a une pile de livres.
Henry has a pile of books.

pillow   l'oreiller (m)

Mimi a un oreiller moelleux.
Mimi has a soft pillow.

---

pilot   le pilote

Un pilote aux commandes d'un avion.
A pilot flying an airplane.

pin   l'épingle (f)

Bill pique Ben avec une épingle.
Bill sticks Ben with a pin.

to pinch   pincer

Bill pince Ben.
Bill pinches Ben.

pineapple   l'ananas (m)

Un gros ananas.
A big pineapple.

pink   rose

Le gros cochon est rose.
The big pig is pink.

---

pipe   la pipe

Ben fume la pipe.
Ben is smoking a pipe.

pitcher   la cruche

Fifi verse le lait de la cruche.
Fifi pours the milk from the pitcher.

place   l'endroit (m)

Ben cherche un endroit où pique-niquer.
Ben is looking for a place to have a picnic.

Elle habite un joli endroit.
She lives in a pretty place.

plant   la plante

Henri tient une plante.
Henry holds a plant.

to plant   planter

Il la plante dans le jardin.
He plants it in the garden.

plate   **l'assiette (f)**

Les frites sont dans une assiette.
The French fries are on a plate.

to play   **jouer**

Les enfants jouent.
The children are playing.

pocket   **la poche**

Le mouchoir est dans la poche.
The handkerchief is in the pocket.

to point   **montrer du doigt**

Ben montre Bill du doigt.
Ben is pointing at Bill.

policeman   **le gendarme**

Le gendarme montre Bill du doigt.
The policeman is pointing at Bill.

to polish   **cirer**

Fritz cire la table.
Fritz is polishing the table.

polite   **poli**

Bill est très poli.
Bill is very polite.

Il est poli de dire s'il vous plaît quand on demande quelque chose.
It is polite to say please when you ask for something.

pond   **la mare**

Des canards nagent sur la mare.
Ducks are swimming in a pond.

pony   **le poney**

Henri monte un poney.
Henry is riding a pony.

poor   **pauvre**

Un homme pauvre a peu d'argent.
A poor man has little money.

porcupine   **le hérisson**

Voici un hérisson.
Here is a porcupine.

pork   **le porc**

Fritz mange du porc.
Fritz is eating pork.

port   **le port**

Le bateau est dans le port.
The ship is in port.

postcard   **la carte postale**

Fifi écrit une carte postale.
Fifi writes a postcard.

post office   **la poste**

Fifi est à la poste.
Fifi is at the post office.

pot   **la casserole**

Ben prend la casserole.
Ben picks up the pot.

potato   **la pomme de terre**

Henri épluche une pomme de terre.
Henry peels a potato.

to pour   **verser**

Henri verse du jus.
Henry is pouring juice.

present   **le cadeau**

Henri donne un cadeau à Fifi.
Henry gives Fifi a present.

to pretend   **faire semblant de**

Fifi fait semblant d'être un fantôme.
Fifi pretends to be a ghost.

pretty   **joli, jolie**

Fifi est une jolie fille.
Fifi is a pretty girl.

price   **le prix**

Quel est le prix des pommes de terre?
What is the price of the potatoes?

prize   **le prix**

Henri a gagné un prix.
Henry has won a prize.

to promise   **promettre**

Fifi a promis d'envoyer une carte postale à Henri.
Fifi has promised to send Henry a postcard.

Je promets de venir.
I promise to come.

pudding   **le pouding**

Mimi aime le pouding.
Mimi likes pudding.

to pull   **tirer**

Bill et Ben tirent sur la corde.
Bill and Ben are pulling the rope.

puppet   **la marionnette**

La marionnette danse.
The puppet is dancing.

puppy   **le chiot**

Un chiot est un bébé chien.
A puppy is a baby dog.

purple   **violet**

Le roi a un manteau violet.
The king has a purple coat.

purse   **le porte-monnaie**

Fifi met de l'argent dans son porte-monnaie.
Fifi puts money in her purse.

to push **pousser**	**queen** **la reine**	**rabbit** **le lapin**

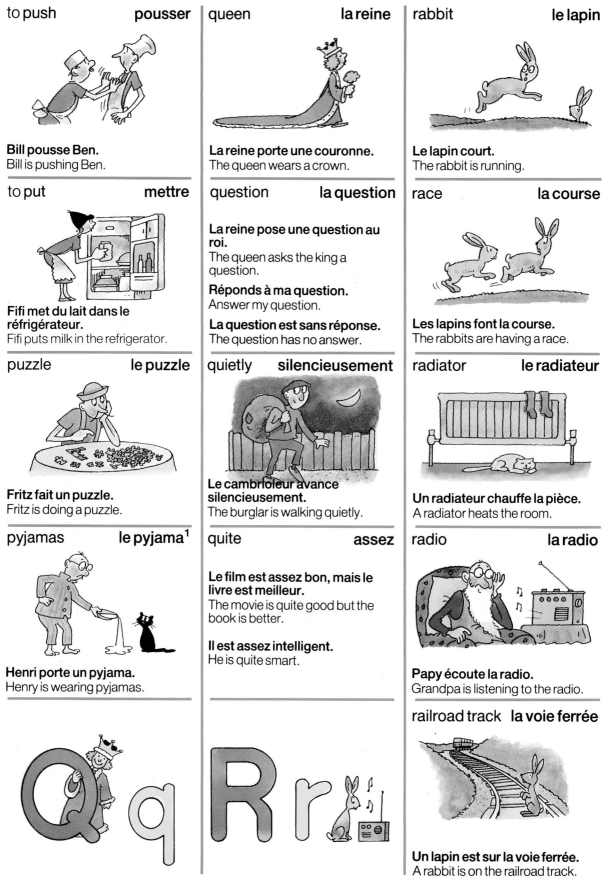

to push   **pousser**

Bill pousse Ben.
Bill is pushing Ben.

to put   **mettre**

Fifi met du lait dans le réfrigérateur.
Fifi puts milk in the refrigerator.

puzzle   **le puzzle**

Fritz fait un puzzle.
Fritz is doing a puzzle.

pyjamas   **le pyjama**[1]

Henri porte un pyjama.
Henry is wearing pyjamas.

queen   **la reine**

La reine porte une couronne.
The queen wears a crown.

question   **la question**

La reine pose une question au roi.
The queen asks the king a question.

Réponds à ma question.
Answer my question.

La question est sans réponse.
The question has no answer.

quietly   **silencieusement**

Le cambrioleur avance silencieusement.
The burglar is walking quietly.

quite   **assez**

Le film est assez bon, mais le livre est meilleur.
The movie is quite good but the book is better.

Il est assez intelligent.
He is quite smart.

rabbit   **le lapin**

Le lapin court.
The rabbit is running.

race   **la course**

Les lapins font la course.
The rabbits are having a race.

radiator   **le radiateur**

Un radiateur chauffe la pièce.
A radiator heats the room.

radio   **la radio**

Papy écoute la radio.
Grandpa is listening to the radio.

railroad track   **la voie ferrée**

Un lapin est sur la voie ferrée.
A rabbit is on the railroad track.

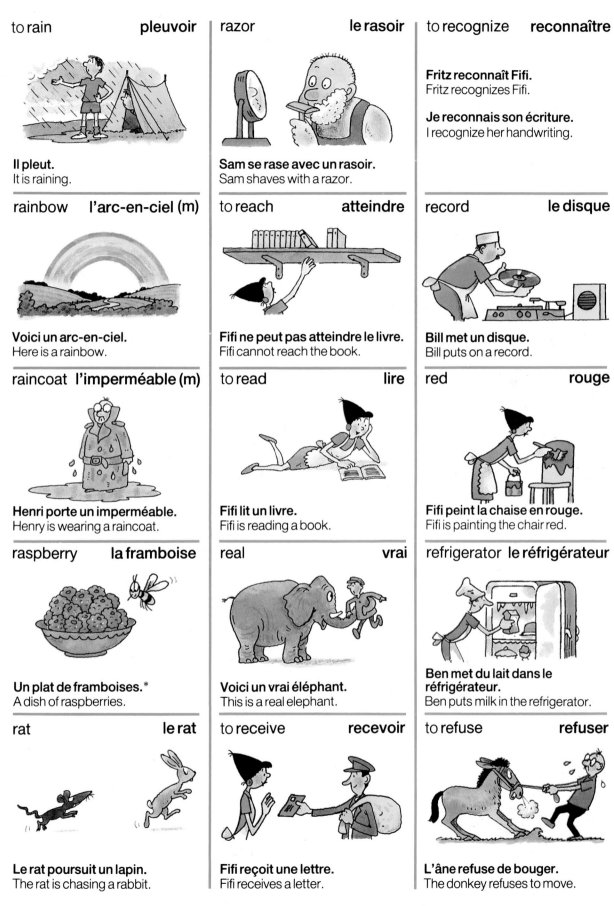

to rain **pleuvoir**	razor **le rasoir**	to recognize **reconnaître**

to rain — **pleuvoir**

Il pleut.
It is raining.

razor — **le rasoir**

Sam se rase avec un rasoir.
Sam shaves with a razor.

to recognize — **reconnaître**

Fritz reconnaît Fifi.
Fritz recognizes Fifi.

Je reconnais son écriture.
I recognize her handwriting.

rainbow — **l'arc-en-ciel (m)**

Voici un arc-en-ciel.
Here is a rainbow.

to reach — **atteindre**

Fifi ne peut pas atteindre le livre.
Fifi cannot reach the book.

record — **le disque**

Bill met un disque.
Bill puts on a record.

raincoat — **l'imperméable (m)**

Henri porte un imperméable.
Henry is wearing a raincoat.

to read — **lire**

Fifi lit un livre.
Fifi is reading a book.

red — **rouge**

Fifi peint la chaise en rouge.
Fifi is painting the chair red.

raspberry — **la framboise**

Un plat de framboises.*
A dish of raspberries.

real — **vrai**

Voici un vrai éléphant.
This is a real elephant.

refrigerator — **le réfrigérateur**

Ben met du lait dans le réfrigérateur.
Ben puts milk in the refrigerator.

rat — **le rat**

Le rat poursuit un lapin.
The rat is chasing a rabbit.

to receive — **recevoir**

Fifi reçoit une lettre.
Fifi receives a letter.

to refuse — **refuser**

L'âne refuse de bouger.
The donkey refuses to move.

to remember	se souvenir de se rappeler de	to ride	monter	road	la route

Fritz se souvient de Fifi.
Fritz remembers Fifi.

Henri ne se rappelle plus où il a mis son livre.
Henry cannot remember where he put his book.

Henri est monté sur âne.
Henry is riding a donkey.

Il y a des moutons sur la route.
There are sheep on the road.

to rest	se reposer	right	droit	to roar	rugir

Henri se repose.
Henry is resting.

Fifi lève la main droite.
Fifi raises her right hand.

Le lion rugit.
The lion is roaring.

ribbon	le ruban	ring	la bague	rock	le rocher

Mimi a un ruban bleu dans les cheveux.
Mimi has a blue ribbon in her hair.

Une bague à la main droite.
A ring on the right hand.

Henri est assis sur un rocher.
Henry is sitting on a rock.

rice	le riz	to ring	sonner	roof	le toit

Les chinois aiment le riz.
The Chinese love rice.

Le téléphone sonne.
The telephone is ringing.

La maison a un toit rouge.
The house has a red roof.

rich	riche	river	la rivière	room	la pièce

Voici un homme riche.
This is a rich man.

La rivière est large.
The river is wide.

Voici une pièce de la maison de Fifi.
This is a room in Fifi's house.

rooster **le coq**	round **rond**	

Le coq chante.
The rooster is calling.

La table est ronde.
The table is round.

root **la racine**

row **la rangée**

sack **le sac**

Cette plante a de longues racines. *
This plant has long roots.

Une rangée de cinq cochons.
Five pigs in a row.

Le voleur porte un grand sac.
The thief is carrying a big sack.

rope **la corde**

to row **ramer**

sad **triste**

Henri grimpe à une corde.
Henry is climbing a rope.

Bill rame.
Bill is rowing.

Henri est triste.
Henry is sad.

rose **la rose**

to rub **se frotter**

safe **sain et sauf**

La rose sent bon.
The rose smells sweet.

Le chat se frotte le dos.
The cat is rubbing its back.

Henri est sain et sauf.
Henry is safe.

rough **mauvais**

to run **courir**

to sail **faire du voilier**

La route est mauvaise.
The road is rough.

Henri court.
Henry is running.

Fifi fait du voilier.
Fifi is sailing.

59

sailboat **le bateau à voiles**

Le bateau à voiles est en mer.
The sailboat is at sea.

sailor **le marin**

Un marin sur son bateau.
A sailor on his boat.

salad **la salade**

Voici une salade.
Here is a salad.

salt **le sel**

Bill met du sel sur la salade.
Bill puts salt on the salad.

same **même**

Deux filles portant le même chapeau.
Two girls wearing the same hat.

sand **le sable**

Mimi creuse un trou dans le sable.
Mimi is digging a hole in the sand.

sandal **la sandale**

Une paire de sandales. *
A pair of sandals.

sandwich **le sandwich**

Un très gros sandwich.
A very big sandwich.

sauce **la sauce**

Fifi verse la sauce.
Fifi is pouring the sauce.

saucer **la soucoupe**

La tasse est sur la soucoupe.
The cup is on the saucer.

sausage **la saucisse**

Ben mange des saucisses. *
Ben is eating sausages.

saw **la scie**

Bill coupe du bois avec une scie.
Bill cuts wood with a saw.

to say **dire**

Bill dit qu'il est riche.
Bill says he is rich.

Leur lettre dit qu'ils vont bien.
The letter says they are well.

Elle dit qu'ils vont venir.
She says they are coming.

scale **la balance**

Fifi est debout sur la balance.
Fifi stands on the scale.

scarf **l'écharpe (f)**

Henri a une très longue écharpe.
Henry has a very long scarf.

| school   l'école (f) | to see   **voir** | sentence   **la phrase** |

Les enfants sont à l'école.
The children are at school.

Mimi voit le phoque.
Mimi sees the seal.

Voici une phrase.
This is a sentence.

| scissors   **les ciseaux (m. pl)** | seed   **la graine** | to serve   **servir** |

Fifi se sert de ciseaux* pour couper les cheveux.
Fifi is using scissors to cut hair.

Dan plante des graines.*
Dan is planting seeds.

Le garçon sert Fifi.
The waiter is serving Fifi.

| to scratch   **se gratter** | to seem   **sembler** | to sew   **coudre** |

Ruff se gratte l'oreille.
Ruff is scratching his ear.

Il semble être en colère.
He seems to be angry.

Henri coud.
Henry is sewing.

| sea   **la mer** | to sell   **vendre** | sewing machine   **la machine à coudre** |

La mer est bleue.
The sea is blue.

Le boulanger vend du pain.
The baker sells bread.

Il se sert d'une machine à coudre.
He is using a sewing machine.

| seal   **le phoque** | to send   **envoyer** | shadow   l'ombre (f) |

Le phoque est dans la mer.
The seal is in the sea.

Fifi envoie une lettre.
Fifi is sending a letter.

Mimi regarde son ombre.
Mimi is looking at her shadow.

to shake **secouer**	shed **la cabane**	shirt **la chemise**

to shake — **secouer**
Bill secoue l'arbre.
Bill is shaking the tree.

shed — **la cabane**
L'ouvrier est dans la cabane.
The workman is in the shed.

shirt — **la chemise**
Fritz a une chemise bleue.
Fritz has a blue shirt.

shape — **la forme**
Voici différentes formes.*
These are different shapes.

sheep — **le mouton**
Trois moutons* en rang.
Three sheep in a row.

shoe — **la chaussure**
Une paire de chaussures* rouges.
A pair of red shoes.

to share — **partager**
Bill et Ben partagent le gâteau.
Bill and Ben share the cake.

sheet — **le drap**
Fifi met un drap sur le lit.
Fifi puts a sheet on the bed.

short — **court**
Le serpent jaune est court.
The yellow snake is short.

shark — **le requin**
Le requin poursuit Henri.
The shark is chasing Henry.

shell — **le coquillage**
Mimi ramasse un coquillage.
Mimi picks up a shell.

shorts — **le short**[1]
Henri porte un short blanc.
Henry is wearing white shorts.

sharp — **aiguisé**
Le couteau est aiguisé.
The knife is sharp.

ship — **le navire**
Le navire est en mer.
The ship is at sea.

shoulder — **l'épaule (f)**
Il y a un oiseau sur l'épaule de Bob.
There is a bird on Bob's shoulder.

1. This word is used in the singular.

shovel	la pelle

Dan bêche avec une pelle.
Dan is digging with a shovel.

to show	montrer

Fifi montre son dessin à Papy.
Fifi shows Grandpa her picture.

shower	la douche

Henri prend une douche.
Henry is taking a shower.

shut	fermé

La barrière est fermée.
The gate is shut.

side	le côté

Un côté de la boîte est rose.
One side of the box is pink.

sidewalk	le trottoir

Fifi est sur le trottoir.
Fifi is on the sidewalk.

sign	l'écriteau (m)

Fred lit un écriteau.
Fred is reading a sign.

silver	l'argent (m)[1]

Fifi a un bracelet d'argent.
Fifi has a silver bracelet.

since	depuis

Fifi n'a pas vu Ben depuis mardi.
Fifi has not seen Ben since
Tuesday.

	puisque

**Puisqu'il fait beau, je vais me
promener.**
Since it is sunny, I will go for a walk.

to sing	chanter

Ces gens chantent.
These people are singing.

sink	le lavabo

Le lavabo est jaune.
The sink is yellow.

sister	la soeur

Mimi et Daisy sont soeurs.*
Mimi and Daisy are sisters.

to sit	être assis

Mimi est assise sur une chaise.
Mimi is sitting on a chair.

to skate	patiner

Fifi et Henri patinent.
Fifi and Henry are skating.

ski	le ski

Henri met des skis.*
Henry puts on skis.

to ski	**faire du ski**	sleeve	**la manche**	slowly	**lentement**

to ski — **faire du ski**

Henri fait du ski.
Henry is skiing.

sleeve — **la manche**

Cette chemise n'a qu'une manche.
This shirt only has one sleeve.

slowly — **lentement**

Un escargot avance lentement.
A snail moves slowly.

skin — **la peau**

Un éléphant a la peau grise.
An elephant has gray skin.

slice — **la tranche**

Bill coupe une tranche de pain.
Bill cuts a slice of bread.

small — **petit**

L'ours brun est petit.
The brown bear is small.

skirt — **la jupe**

Fifi porte une jupe rouge.
Fifi is wearing a red skirt.

to slide — **glisser**

Henri glisse sur la glace.
Henry is sliding on the ice.

to smell — **sentir**

Fifi sent le parfum.
Fifi smells the perfume.

sky — **le ciel**

L'oiseau est dans le ciel.
The bird is in the sky.

slide — **la diapositive**

Voici une diapositive.
This is a slide.

to smile — **sourire**

Fifi sourit.
Fifi is smiling.

to sleep — **dormir**

Mimi dort.
Mimi is sleeping.

slipper — **la pantoufle**

Mimi a des pantoufles* rouges.
Mimi has red slippers.

to smoke — **fumer**

Papy fume la pipe.
Grandpa is smoking a pipe.

64

snail	l'escargot (m)

Revoici l'escargot.
Here is the snail again.

sock	la chaussette

Mimi porte des chaussettes* roses.
Mimi is wearing pink socks.

someone	quelqu'un

Quelqu'un a volé ma voiture.
Someone has stolen my car.

something	quelque chose

J'ai quelque chose dans l'oeil.
There is something in my eye.

sometimes	quelquefois

Quelquefois je suis triste.
Sometimes I am sad.

snake	le serpent

Le serpent est dans l'herbe.
The snake is in the grass.

sofa	le canapé

Fifi est assise sur le canapé.
Fifi is sitting on the sofa.

son	le fils

Henri est le fils de Papy.
Henry is Grandpa's son.

to snow	neiger

Il neige.
It is snowing.

soft	moelleux, moelleuse

Le coussin est moelleux.
The cushion is soft.

song	la chanson

La chanteuse chante une chanson.
The singer is singing a song.

soap	le savon

Ben a du savon sur la figure.
Ben has soap on his face.

soldier	le soldat

Le soldat est dans l'armée.
The soldier is in the army.

soon	bientôt

Nous rentrerons bientôt à la maison.
We will go home soon.

A bientôt!
I'll see you soon!

soccer	le football

Sam joue au football.
Sam plays soccer.

some	certain

Certains soldats sourient.
Some soldiers are smiling.

sort	la sorte

Trois sortes* de chapeaux.
Three sorts of hats.

soup	**la soupe**

Henri mange de la soupe.
Henry is eating soup.

to spend	**dépenser**

Ben dépense de l'argent.
Ben is spending money.

square	**le carré**

Voici un carré.
Here is a square.

south	**le sud**

L'oiseau regarde vers le sud.
The bird is facing South.

spider	**l'araignée (f)**

L'araignée fait peur à Fifi.
The spider frightens Fifi.

stable	**l'écurie (f)**

Le cheval vit dans une écurie.
The horse lives in a stable.

space	**l'espace (m)**

L'astronaute est dans l'espace.
The astronaut is in space.

spoon	**la cuiller**

Mimi mange avec une cuiller.
Mimi is eating with a spoon.

stairs	**l'escalier (m)**[1]

Mimi monte l'escalier.
Mimi is going up the stairs.

to speak	**parler**

Fifi parle à Papy.
Fifi is speaking to Grandpa.

spot	**la tache**

Mimi a beaucoup de taches* rouges.
Mimi has lots of red spots.

stamp	**le timbre**

Deux timbres* sur une enveloppe.
Two stamps on an envelope.

to spell	**épeler**

Mimi sait épeler son nom.
Mimi can spell her name.

to spread	**étaler**

Bill étale le beurre.
Bill is spreading the butter.

to stand	**se tenir debout**

Bill se tient debout sur le dos de Ben.
Bill is standing on Ben's back.

star	l'étoile (f)	to steal	voler	stockings	les bas (m. pl)

star   l'étoile (f)

L'étoile brille dans le ciel.
The star shines in the sky.

to steal   voler

Fred vole des bijoux.
Fred is stealing jewels.

stockings   les bas (m. pl)

Fifi a des bas* noirs.
Fifi has black stockings.

to start   commencer

La course commence.
The race is starting.

stem   la tige

La fleur a une longue tige.
The flower has a long stem.

stone   la pierre

Mimi ramasse une pierre.
Mimi picks up a stone.

station   la gare

Le train est en gare.
The train is in the station.

step   la marche

Le chat est assis sur la marche.
The cat is sitting on the step.

to stop   s'arrêter

La voiture s'arrête au feu rouge.
The car stops at the red light.

statue   la statue

Henri regarde une statue.
Henry is looking at a statue.

stereo   la chaîne stéréo

Voici une chaîne stéréo.
This is a stereo.

store   le magasin

Fifi entre dans un magasin.
Fifi goes into a store.

to stay   rester

Reste ici!
Stay here!

Fifi reste au lit.
Fifi stays in bed.

Henri doit rester quatre jours à Paris.
Henry has to stay in Paris for 4 days.

stick   le bâton

Dan porte des bâtons.*
Dan is carrying sticks.

storm   l'orage (m)

Voici un orage.
This is a storm.

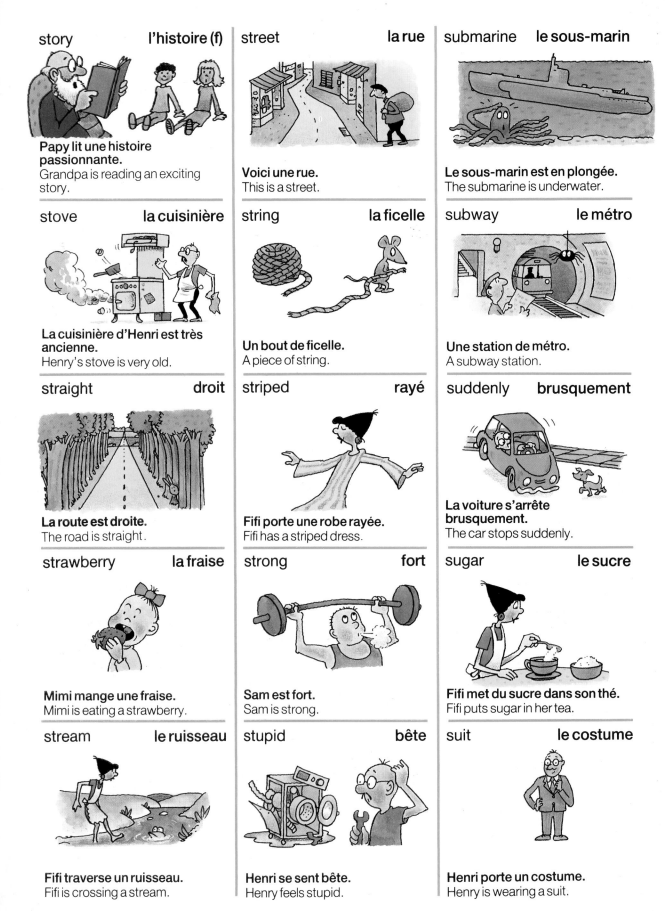

story — l'histoire (f)

Papy lit une histoire passionnante.
Grandpa is reading an exciting story.

street — la rue

Voici une rue.
This is a street.

submarine — le sous-marin

Le sous-marin est en plongée.
The submarine is underwater.

stove — la cuisinière

La cuisinière d'Henri est très ancienne.
Henry's stove is very old.

string — la ficelle

Un bout de ficelle.
A piece of string.

subway — le métro

Une station de métro.
A subway station.

straight — droit

La route est droite.
The road is straight.

striped — rayé

Fifi porte une robe rayée.
Fifi has a striped dress.

suddenly — brusquement

La voiture s'arrête brusquement.
The car stops suddenly.

strawberry — la fraise

Mimi mange une fraise.
Mimi is eating a strawberry.

strong — fort

Sam est fort.
Sam is strong.

sugar — le sucre

Fifi met du sucre dans son thé.
Fifi puts sugar in her tea.

stream — le ruisseau

Fifi traverse un ruisseau.
Fifi is crossing a stream.

stupid — bête

Henri se sent bête.
Henry feels stupid.

suit — le costume

Henri porte un costume.
Henry is wearing a suit.

suitcase	**la valise**

Ben porte une valise.
Ben is carrying a suitcase.

to swallow	**avaler**

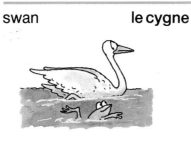

Le serpent avale quelque chose.
The snake swallows something.

swimsuit	**le maillot de bain**

Fifi porte un maillot de bain rayé.
Fifi wears a striped swimsuit.

sun	**le soleil**

Le soleil brille.
The sun is shining.

swan	**le cygne**

Le cygne nage.
The swan is swimming.

swing	**la balançoire**

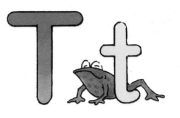

Ben est sur une balançoire.
Ben is on a swing.

supermarket	**le supermarché**

Fifi est au supermarché.
Fifi is at the supermarket.

sweater	**le chandail**

Aggie porte un chandail rose.
Aggie is wearing a pink sweater.

table	**la table**

Quelle surprise pour Fifi!
What a surprise for Fifi!

to swim	**nager**

Bill et Ben nagent.
Bill and Ben are swimming.

Le chat est sur la table.
The cat is on the table.

to surround	**entourer**

swimming pool	**la piscine**

tail	**la queue**

Les oiseaux entourent le chat.
The birds surround the cat.

Voici la piscine.
This is the swimming pool.

Un seul chat a une queue.
Only one cat has a tail.

to take   **prendre**

Mimi prend un chocolat.
Mimi takes a chocolate.

tall   **grand**

La dame est grande.
The woman is tall.

to taste   **goûter**

Ben goûte la sauce.
Ben is tasting the sauce.

taxi   **le taxi**

Fritz appelle un taxi.
Fritz calls a taxi.

tea   **le thé**

Fifi prend une tasse de thé.
Fifi has a cup of tea.

teacher   **le professeur**

Le professeur fait la classe.
The teacher is teaching the class.

team   **l'équipe (f)**

Une équipe de football.
A soccer team.

teapot   **la théière**

Fifi verse du thé d'une théière.
Fifi pours tea from a teapot.

to tear   **déchirer**

Henri déchire son pantalon.
Henry tears his pants.

tear   **la larme**

Mimi a des larmes* sur la figure.
Mimi has tears on her face.

teddy bear   **l'ours en peluche (m)**

Mimi a un ours en peluche.
Mimi has a teddy bear.

teeth   **les dents (f. pl)**

Le rat a des dents* pointues.
The rat has sharp teeth.

telephone   **le téléphone**

Le téléphone sonne.
The telephone is ringing.

television   **la télévision**

Les enfants regardent la télévision.
The children are watching television.

to tell   **raconter**

Papy raconte une histoire aux enfants.
Grandpa is telling the children a story.

tennis   **le tennis**

Ces hommes jouent au tennis.
These men are playing tennis.

then   **puis**

Il a dîné, puis il a mangé un morceau de gâteau.
He ate his dinner, then he had a piece of cake.

Mets un timbre sur la lettre, puis poste-la.
Put a stamp on the letter, then mail it.

thing   **la chose**

Plusieurs choses* sur un plateau.
Several things on a tray.

tent   **la tente**

Henri met la tête hors de la tente.
Henry looks out of the tent.

there   **là**

Est-ce que Fifi est là?
Is Fifi there?

Ne bouge pas de là.
Do not move from there.

to think   **penser**

Fifi pense à Sam.
Fifi is thinking about Sam.

to thank   **remercier**

Fifi remercie Ben de son cadeau.
Fifi thanks Ben for the present.

thick   **épais, épaisse**

La tranche de pain est épaisse.
The slice of bread is thick.

to be thirsty   **avoir soif**

Cet homme a soif.
This man is thirsty.

that   **ce, cette, cet, ces*[1]**
Donne-moi ce chapeau.
Give me that hat.

Donne-moi cette pomme.
Give me that apple.

thief   **le voleur**

this   **ce, cette, cet, ces*[1]**

Prends ce chapeau.
Take this hat.

that is   **voilà**

Voilà ma soeur!
That is my sister!

Voilà mon frère!
That is my brother!

Le voleur vole des bijoux.
The thief is stealing jewels.

this is   **voici**

Voici un éléphant.
This is an elephant.

theater   **le théâtre**

thin   **maigre**

thread   **le fil**

Fifi est au théâtre.
Fifi is at the theater.

Cet homme est maigre.
This man is thin.

Fifi coud avec du fil de coton.
Fifi is sewing with cotton thread.

1. **Ce, cette, cet, ces** mean either "this" or "that." **Cet** is used before masculine singular nouns that begin with a vowel; **cet arbre** = "this tree" or "that tree." **Ces** is used with *all* plural nouns; **ces hommes** = "these men" or "those men"; **ces femmes** = "these women" or "those women."

through **par**	to tie (a knot) **faire un noeud**	to **à**

through — **par**

Le roi entre par la porte.
The king comes in through the door.

to tie (a knot) — **faire un noeud**

Bill fait un noeud.
Bill is tying a knot.

to — **à**

Les enfants vont à l'école.
The children go to school.

Henri va à la gare.
Henry is going to the train station.

Bill donne une pomme à Ben.
Bill gives an apple to Ben.

to throw — **jeter**

Mimi jette du pain aux canards.
Mimi is throwing bread to the ducks.

tiger — **le tigre**

Le tigre rugit.
The tiger is roaring.

today — **aujourd'hui**

Aujourd'hui, c'est l'anniversaire de Mimi.
Today is Mimi's birthday.

thumb — **le pouce**

Henri se tape sur le pouce.
Henry hits his thumb.

tights — **le collant**[1]

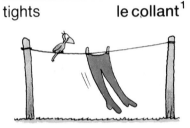

Un collant rouge.
Red tights.

toe — **l'orteil (m)**

La souris chatouille les orteils* de Sam.
The mouse is tickling Sam's toes.

ticket — **le billet**

Fifi montre son billet.
Fifi shows her ticket.

tire — **le pneu**

Les pneus* de la bicyclette sont à plat.
The bicycle has flat tires.

together — **ensemble**

Les chats dorment ensemble.
The cats sleep together.

tie — **la cravate**

Henri a une cravate à pois.
Henry has a spotted tie.

tired — **fatigué**

Henri est fatigué.
Henry is tired.

tomato — **la tomate**

Henri coupe des tomates.*
Henry is slicing tomatoes.

1. This word is used in the singular.

tomorrow	**demain**

Demain est le jour qui suit aujourd'hui.
Tomorrow is the day after today.

Aujourd'hui c'est lundi, alors demain ce sera mardi.
Today is Monday so tomorrow will be Tuesday.

tongue	**la langue**

Ruff a une langue rose.
Ruff has a pink tongue.

too	**trop**

La veste est trop petite.
The jacket is too small.

tool	**l'outil (m)**

Voici des outils.*
Here are some tools.

toothbrush	**la brosse à dents**

Une brosse à dents jaune.
A yellow toothbrush.

toothpaste	**le dentifrice**

Du dentifrice sur une brosse à dents.
Toothpaste on a toothbrush.

top	**le haut**

Ben est en haut de l'escabeau.
Ben is at the top of the stepladder.

to touch	**toucher**

Qui touche l'épaule du voleur?
Who touches the thief's shoulder?

towards	**vers**

Le chat se dirige vers son lait.
The cat goes towards his milk.

towel	**la serviette**

Henri a une serviette jaune.
Henry has a yellow towel.

tower	**la tour**

Où se trouve cette célèbre tour?
Where is this famous tower?

town	**la ville**

Voici une ville.
This is a town.

toy	**le jouet**

Mimi s'amuse avec un jouet.
Mimi is playing with a toy.

tractor	**le tracteur**

Henri conduit un tracteur.
Henry is driving a tractor.

traffic lights	**les feux (m. pl)**

Il est rentré dans les feux.*
He has hit the traffic lights.

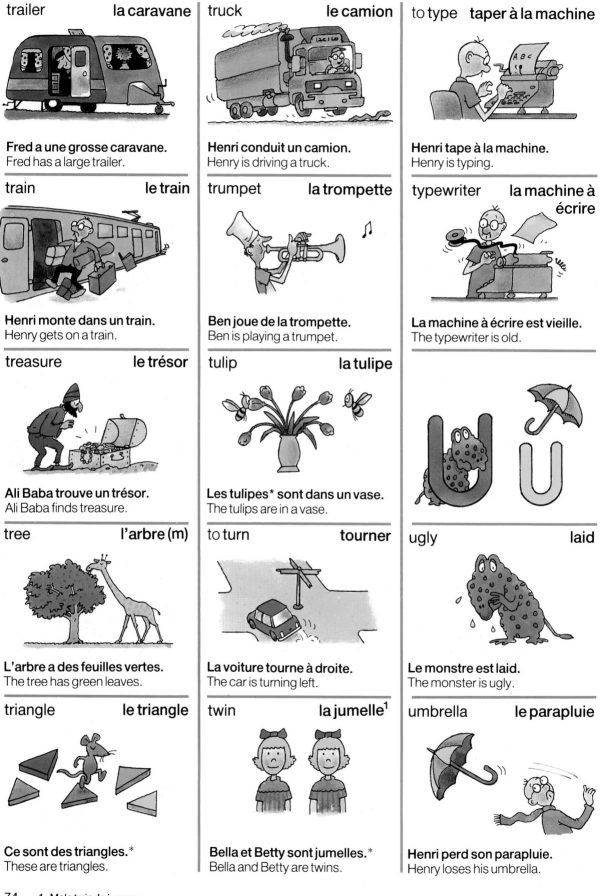

trailer   **la caravane**

Fred a une grosse caravane.
Fred has a large trailer.

train   **le train**

Henri monte dans un train.
Henry gets on a train.

treasure   **le trésor**

Ali Baba trouve un trésor.
Ali Baba finds treasure.

tree   **l'arbre (m)**

L'arbre a des feuilles vertes.
The tree has green leaves.

triangle   **le triangle**

Ce sont des triangles. *
These are triangles.

truck   **le camion**

Henri conduit un camion.
Henry is driving a truck.

trumpet   **la trompette**

Ben joue de la trompette.
Ben is playing a trumpet.

tulip   **la tulipe**

Les tulipes* sont dans un vase.
The tulips are in a vase.

to turn   **tourner**

La voiture tourne à droite.
The car is turning left.

twin   **la jumelle**[1]

Bella et Betty sont jumelles. *
Bella and Betty are twins.

to type   **taper à la machine**

Henri tape à la machine.
Henry is typing.

typewriter   **la machine à écrire**

La machine à écrire est vieille.
The typewriter is old.

ugly   **laid**

Le monstre est laid.
The monster is ugly.

umbrella   **le parapluie**

Henri perd son parapluie.
Henry loses his umbrella.

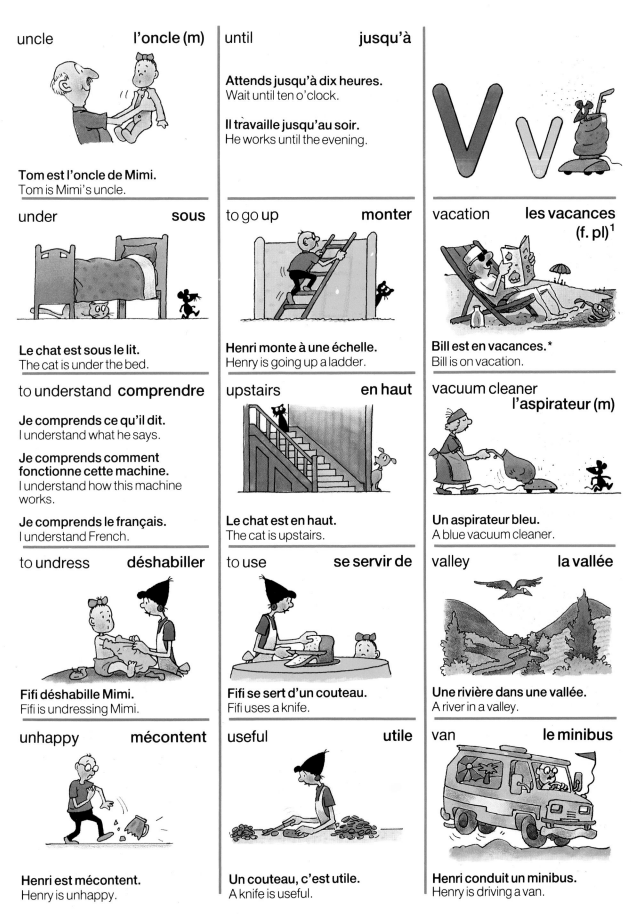

uncle　　　　　l'oncle (m)

Tom est l'oncle de Mimi.
Tom is Mimi's uncle.

under　　　　　sous

Le chat est sous le lit.
The cat is under the bed.

to understand　**comprendre**

Je comprends ce qu'il dit.
I understand what he says.

**Je comprends comment
fonctionne cette machine.**
I understand how this machine
works.

Je comprends le français.
I understand French.

to undress　　**déshabiller**

Fifi déshabille Mimi.
Fifi is undressing Mimi.

unhappy　　　**mécontent**

Henri est mécontent.
Henry is unhappy.

until　　　　　jusqu'à

Attends jusqu'à dix heures.
Wait until ten o'clock.

Il travaille jusqu'au soir.
He works until the evening.

to go up　　　**monter**

Henri monte à une échelle.
Henry is going up a ladder.

upstairs　　　**en haut**

Le chat est en haut.
The cat is upstairs.

to use　　　**se servir de**

Fifi se sert d'un couteau.
Fifi uses a knife.

useful　　　　**utile**

Un couteau, c'est utile.
A knife is useful.

V v

vacation　　**les vacances
(f. pl)**[1]

Bill est en vacances.*
Bill is on vacation.

vacuum cleaner
　　　　l'aspirateur (m)

Un aspirateur bleu.
A blue vacuum cleaner.

valley　　　　**la vallée**

Une rivière dans une vallée.
A river in a valley.

van　　　　　**le minibus**

Henri conduit un minibus.
Henry is driving a van.

---

1. The word for 'vacation' is always plural in French.

| vase | **le vase** | to visit | **rendre visite à** | to wake up | **se réveiller** |

Le vase est plein de fleurs.
The vase is full of flowers.

| vegetable | **le légume** |

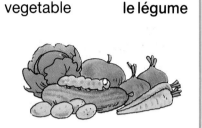

Voici des légumes. *
Here are some vegetables.

| very | **très** |

La jeune fille est très jolie.
The girl is very pretty.

Henri parle très bien le français.
Henry speaks French very well.

Très bien!
Very good!

| village | **le village** |

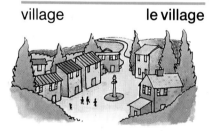

Un village est une petite ville.
A village is a small town.

| violin | **le violon** |

Henri joue du violon.
Henry plays the violin.

Fifi rend visite à Papy.
Fifi is visiting Grandpa.

| voice | **la voix** |

Papy a une voix douce.
Grandpa has a quiet voice.

Ben a la voix grave et Fifi a la voix aigüe.
Ben has a low voice and Fifi has a high voice.

| to wait | **attendre** |

Aggie attend l'autobus.
Aggie is waiting for the bus.

| waiter | **le garçon** |

Le garçon sert Fifi.
The waiter serves Fifi.

Henri se réveille.
Henry is waking up.

| walk | **la promenade** |

Fifi fait une promenade.
Fifi is going for a walk.

| wall | **le mur** |

Les chats sont sur le mur.
The cats are on the wall.

| wallpaper | **le papier peint** |

Bill pose du papier peint.
Bill is putting up wallpaper.

| to want | **vouloir** |

Mimi veut un petit gâteau.
Mimi wants a cupcake.

war	la guerre

Ces deux pays sont en guerre.
The two countries are at war.

La guerre a duré deux ans.
The war has lasted two years.

watch	la montre

Fifi regarde sa montre.
Fifi looks at her watch.

to wear	porter

Fifi porte un chapeau.
Fifi is wearing a hat.

warm	chaud

Fifi a chaud.
Fifi is warm.

water	l'eau (f)

La baignoire est pleine d'eau.
The bathtub is full of water.

wedding	le mariage

Un mariage à l'église.
A wedding at the church.

to wash	se laver

Henri se lave la figure.
Henry is washing his face.

waterfall	la chute d'eau

Tarzan franchit la chute d'eau.
Tarzan crosses the waterfall.

to weigh	peser

Fifi pèse la farine.
Fifi weighs the flour.

washing machine	la machine à laver

La machine à laver est en marche.
The washing machine is on.

wave	la vague

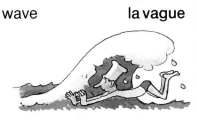

Ben plonge sous la vague.
Ben dives under the wave.

west	l'ouest (m)

L'oiseau regarde vers l'ouest.
The bird is facing west.

wasp	la guêpe

La guêpe a piqué Henri.
The wasp has stung Henry.

weak	faible

Henri est faible.
Henry is weak.

wet	mouillé

Le chien est mouillé.
The dog is wet.

what	que

Que veux-tu pour le déjeuner?
What would you like for lunch?

Que dis-tu? Je ne comprends pas.
What are you saying? I do not understand.

where	où

Où est le chat?
Where is the cat?

white	blanc, blanche

Le gros chat est blanc.
The fat cat is white.

wheat	le blé

Le blé pousse dans le champ.
The wheat is growing in the field.

which	quel, quelle

Quel est le plus gros chat?
Which cat is the biggest?

who	qui

Qui porte un chapeau?
Who is wearing a hat?

wheel	la roue

Une bicyclette a deux roues.*
A bicycle has two wheels.

while	pendant que

Mimi rêve pendant qu'elle dort.
Mimi dreams while she sleeps.

why	pourquoi

Pourquoi Henri est-il dans l'arbre?
Why is Henry up a tree?

wheelbarrow	la brouette

La brouette est pleine.
The wheelbarrow is full.

to whisper	chuchoter

Fifi chuchote quelque chose à Ben.
Fifi is whispering to Ben.

wide	large

La rivière est très large.
The river is very wide.

when	quand

Quand part le dernier train?
When does the last train leave?

J'avais une voiture quand j'habitais à Paris.
I had a car when I lived in Paris.

Viens quand tu auras fini.
Come when you have finished.

whistle	le sifflet

L'homme donne un coup de sifflet.
The man is blowing a whistle.

wife	la femme

Heidi est la femme de Fritz.
Heidi is Fritz's wife.

to win **gagner**	to wipe **essuyer**	woman **la femme**
Sam gagne la course. Sam wins the race.	**Bill essuie la table.** Bill is wiping the table.	**Fifi est une femme. Henri est un homme.** Fifi is a woman. Henry is a man.
wind **le vent**	wire **le fil de fer**	wood **le bois**
Le vent souffle. The wind is blowing.	**La clôture est en fil de fer.** The fence is made of wire.	**La table est en bois.** The table is made of wood.
windmill **le moulin à vent**	witch **la sorcière**	wool **la laine**
Voici un moulin à vent. This is a windmill.	**La sorcière vole.** The witch is flying.	**Trois pelotes de laine.** Three balls of wool.
window **la vitre**[1]	with **avec**	word **le mot**
Le voleur casse la vitre. The thief breaks the window.	**La sorcière est avec son chat.** The witch is with her cat.	**Mimi écrit un mot.** Mimi is writing a word.
wing **l'aile (f)**	without **sans**	to work **travailler**
L'oiseau bat des ailes. * The bird flaps its wings.	**La sorcière est sans son chat.** The witch is without her cat.	**Ben travaille dur.** Ben is working hard.

1. **La vitre** is the word for the window pane. The word for window is **la fenêtre.**

workbook — le livre d'exercices

Tim écrit dans son livre d'exercices.
Tim is writing in his workbook.

world — le monde

Voici une carte du monde.
This is a map of the world.

worm — le ver de terre

L'oiseau regarde le ver de terre.
The bird looks at the worm.

to wrap — emballer

Fifi emballe un cadeau.
Fifi is wrapping a present.

to write — écrire

Fifi écrit une lettre.
Fifi is writing a letter.

wrong — faux, fausse

La solution est fausse.
The answer is wrong.

Y y

year — l'année (f)

Il y a 365 jours dans l'année.
There are 365 days in a year.

Il y a 12 mois ou 52 semaines dans l'année.
There are 12 months or 52 weeks in a year.

to yell — crier

Ben crie à Bill.
Ben is yelling at Bill.

yellow — jaune

Le poussin est jaune.
The chick is yellow.

yesterday — hier

Hier est le jour qui a précédé aujourd'hui.
Yesterday was the day before today.

Aujourd'hui c'est lundi, hier c'était dimanche.
Today is Monday, yesterday was Sunday.

young — jeune

Un chiot est un jeune chien.
A puppy is a young dog.

Z z

zebra — le zèbre

Un zèbre a un pelage rayé.
A zebra has a striped coat.

zoo — le zoo

Mimi regarde un zèbre au zoo.
Mimi sees a zebra at the zoo.

Pronunciation Guide

In French, many letters are pronounced differently from the way they are said in English. The best way to learn to speak French is to listen carefully to French-speaking people and copy what they say, but here are some general pointers to help you.

Below is a list of letters, with a guide to show you how to pronounce each one. For each French sound, we show an English word (or part of a word) that sounds like it. Read it out loud normally to find out how to pronounce the French sound, then practice saying the examples shown below.

a
Often like the "a" sound in "cart":
arriver, Paris, chat, mari

e
Like the "a" sound in "above":
le, petit, regarder

é
Like the "ay" sound in "late":
été, café, thé

è
Like the "a" sound in "care":
mère, père

ê
Like the "e" sound in "get":
même, vous êtes

i
Like the "i" in "machine":
il, dix, police, ville

o
Like the "o" in "holiday":
fromage, pomme

u
Round your lips as if you were going to say "oo," then try to say "ee": du, une, plus, musique

eau, au
Like the "oa" sound in "toast":
eau, beau, gauche, château

eu
Like the "u" sound in "fur":
deux, bleu, cheveu

ou
Like the "oo" sound in "food":
ou, tout, beacoup

oi
Like the "wa" sound in "what":
voix, poisson, boîte

on, an
Like "ong" without the "g" sound at the end:
dans, bonjour, français, Avignon

un
Like the "u" sound in "sun." You do not pronounce the "n":
un, chacun

in, ain, im
Like the "an" sound in "rang" without the "g" at the end:
vin, prince, impossible, train

c
Before "i" or "e," it sounds like the "s" in "sun":
merci, France, certain

Before other letters, it sounds like the "c" in "cat":
café, cotton, crabe

ç
Like the "s" in "sun":
garçon, français

ch
Like the "sh" sound in "shirt":
cochon, vache, chanter, Charles

g
Before "i" or "e," it sounds like the "s" sound in "measure":
gendarme, girafe, âge

Before other letters, it is like the "g" in "get":
grand, gare, guitare

gn
Like the "ni" sound in "onion":
campagne, montagne

j
Like the "s" sound in "measure":
bonjour, jeune

th
Like the "t" in "top":
thé, théâtre

qu
Like the "k" sound in "kettle":
question, musique

h
This letter is not pronounced:
histoire, hôpital, hôtel

A consonant at the end of a French word is not usually pronounced: français, petit, les, tout.

Basic Grammar

French grammar is different from English grammar. These notes on basic grammar will help you understand some of the things you come across in the French sentences in this dictionary.

the

In French every noun is masculine or feminine. The word you use for "the" shows whether the noun is masculine or feminine and also whether it is singular or plural. The word for "the" is **le** before masculine nouns, **la** before feminine nouns and **l'** before all singular nouns beginning with a vowel.

le livre	the book
la maison	the house
l'arbre	the tree

The word for "the" is **les** before all plural nouns:

les livres	the books
les maisons	the houses
les arbres	the trees

If **le** comes after **à** (to, at) it becomes **au**:

Fifi va au cinéma
Fifi goes to the movies

les after **à** becomes **aux**:

Ben donne les os aux chiens
Ben gives the bones to the dogs

If **le** comes after **de** (of), it becomes **du**:

le chien du boulanger
the dog of the baker

les after **de** becomes **des**:

la mère des enfants
the mother of the children

a, an

The French for "a" or "an" is **un** before masculine nouns and **une** before feminine nouns:

un livre	a book
une maison	a house
un arbre	a tree

some, any

The French for "some" or "any" is **du** before a masculine noun, **de la** before a feminine noun, **de l'** before singular nouns beginning with a vowel and **des** before plural nouns.

du lait	some milk
de la glace	some ice cream
de l'eau	some water
des pommes	some apples

Pronouns

The French word for "it" or "they" depends on whether the noun it replaces is masculine or feminine. "It" may be **il** or **elle**; "they" may be **ils** or **elles**.

le chat dort	**il dort**
the cat sleeps	it sleeps

les vaches dorment	**elles dorment**
the cows sleep	they sleep

The subject pronouns in French are:

I	je	we	nous
you*	tu	you *	vous
he/it (m)	il	they (m)	ils
she/it (f)	elle	they (f)	elles

Possessives

The word you use for "my," "your," "his," etc., depends on whether the word that follows it is masculine, feminine, or plural.

mon livre	my book
ma maison	my house
mes frères	my brothers

	(m)	(f)	(pl)
my	**mon**	**ma**	**mes**
your*	**ton**	**ta**	**tes**
his/her/its	**son**	**sa**	**ses**
our	**notre**	**notre**	**nos**
your *	**votre**	**votre**	**vos**
their	**leur**	**leur**	**leurs**

* **tu, ta, ton** and **tes** are singular informal; **vous** is formal and may refer to one or several persons; **votre** and **vos** are both formal, but **votre** goes before singular nouns and **vos** before plural nouns.

Adjectives

French adjectives are masculine or feminine to go with the nouns they are describing. You usually add "e" to a masculine singular adjective to make it feminine, unless the adjective already ends in "e."

le petit chien	the little dog
la petite chaise	the little chair
le livre vert	the green book
la robe verte	the green dress

You usually add "s" to an adjective to make it plural.

les petits chiens	the little dogs
les petites chaises	the little chairs
les livres verts	the green books
les robes vertes	the green dresses

Most French adjectives follow the noun, but some common ones, such as **petit** (little), **bon** (good), and **jeune** (young), come before the noun.

Verbs

The ending of a French verb changes depending on the subject. There are three main types of verbs: those ending in **er**, those ending in **ir**, and those ending in **re**. Most French verbs follow the pattern of one of these types of verbs.

parler	to speak
je parle	I speak
tu parles	you speak*
il/elle parle	he/she/it speaks
nous parlons	we speak
vous parlez	you speak *
ils/elles parlent	they speak

finir	to finish
je finis	I finish
tu finis	you finish*
il/elle finit	he/she/it finishes
nous finissons	we finish
vous finissez	you finish *
ils/elles finissent	they finish

vendre	to sell
je vends	I sell
tu vends	you sell*
il/elle vend	he/she/it sells
nous vendons	we sell
vous vendez	you sell*
ils/elles vendent	they sell

Here are some useful verbs that do not follow these regular patterns.

être	to be
je suis	I am
tu es	you are
il/elle est	he/she/it is
nous sommes	we are
vous êtes	you are
ils/elles sont	they are

avoir	to have
j'ai	I have
tu as	you have
il/elle a	he/she/it has
nous avons	we have
vous avez	you have
ils/elles ont	they have

aller	to go
je vais	I go
tu vas	you go
il/elle va	he/she/it goes
nous allons	we go
vous allez	you go
ils/elles vont	they go

Reflexive verbs

These are verbs that always have a special pronoun in front of them. Where in English we say "I get up," the French say "I get myself up" **Je me lève**. The pronoun changes depending on the subject of the verb:

se lever	to get up
je me lève	I get up
tu te lèves	you get up
il/elle se lève	he/she/it gets up
nous nous levons	we get up
vous vous levez	you get up
ils/elles se lèvent	they get up

Useful Words and Phrases

Months, Seasons, and Days

The French names for the days of the week, the months of the year and the seasons are all masculine. None of them begin with a capital letter.

The months

January	janvier
February	février
March	mars
April	avril
May	mai
June	juin
July	juillet
August	août
September	septembre
October	octobre
November	novembre
December	décembre

The seasons

spring	le printemps
summer	l'été
autumn/fall	l'automne
winter	l'hiver

The days

Monday	lundi
Tuesday	mardi
Wednesday	mercredi
Thursday	jeudi
Friday	vendredi
Saturday	samedi
Sunday	dimanche

Numbers and Telling Time

1	un	13	treize	32	trente-deux	80	quatre-vingts
2	deux	14	quatorze	40	quarante	81	quatre-vingt-un
3	trois	15	quinze	50	cinquante	90	quatre-vingt-dix
4	quatre	16	seize	60	soixante	91	quatre-vingt-onze
5	cinq	17	dix-sept	70	soixante-dix	92	quatre-vingt-douze
6	six	18	dix-huit	71	soixante et onze	100	cent
7	sept	19	dix-neuf	72	soixante-douze	101	cent un
8	huit	20	vingt	73	soixante-treize	150	cent cinquante
9	neuf	21	vingt et un	74	soixante-quatorze	200	deux cents
10	dix	22	vingt-deux	75	soixante-quinze	201	deux cent un
11	onze	30	trente	76	soixante-seize	500	cinq cents
12	douze	31	trente et un	77	soixante-dix-sept	1000	mille

Telling time

What time is it?	Quelle heure est-il?
It is nine o'clock	Il est neuf heures
It is five after nine	Il est neuf heures cinq
It is a quarter after nine	Il est neuf heures et quart
It is half past nine	Il est neuf heures et demie
It is a quarter to ten	Il est dix heures moins le quart
It is five to ten	Il est dix heures moins cinq
It is noon/midnight	Il est midi/minuit

Countries and Continents

Africa	l'Afrique (f)	India	l'Inde (f)
Algeria	l'Algérie (f)	Italy	l'Italie (f)
Asia	l'Asie (f)	Japan	le Japon
Australia	l'Australie (f)	Mexico	le Mexique
Austria	l'Autriche (f)	The Netherlands	les Pays Bas (m. pl)
Belgium	la Belgique	New Zealand	la Nouvelle-Zélande
Brazil	le Brésil	North America	l'Amérique du Nord (f)
Canada	le Canada	Poland	la Pologne
China	la Chine	Quebec	le Québec
Denmark	le Danemark	Senegal	le Sénégal
England	l'Angleterre (f)	South America	l'Amérique du Sud
Europe	l'Europe (f)	Soviet Union	l'Union soviétique (f)
France	la France	Spain	l'Espagne (f)
Germany	l'Allemagne (f)	Switzerland	la Suisse
Great Britain	la Grande Bretagne	United States	les Etats-Unis (m. pl)

Useful Words and Phrases

Yes	Oui
No	Non
Please	S'il vous plaît
I would like . . .	Je voudrais . . .
Thank you	Merci
I'm sorry	Pardon
Excuse me	Excusez-moi
Mr.	Monsieur
Mrs.	Madame
Miss	Mademoiselle
I do not understand.	Je ne comprends pas.
I do not speak French.	Je ne parle pas français.
Please speak more slowly.	Plus lentement, s'il vous plaît.

Making friends

Hello	Bonjour
Good evening	Bonsoir
Good night	Bonne nuit
Goodbye	Au revoir
What is your name?	Comment t'appelles-tu?
My name is Roger.	Je m'appelle Roger.
How are you?	Comment vas-tu?
I am well, thank you.	Je vais bien, merci.

Asking for directions

Where is . . . ?	Où est . . . ?
Where are . . . ?	Où sont . . . ?
How do I get to the train station please?	Pour aller à la gare s'il vous plaît?
You go . . .	Vous allez . . .
You continue . . .	Vous continuez . . .
You turn . . .	Vous tournez . . .
to the right	à droite
to the left	à gauche
straight ahead	tout droit

Useful places to ask for

airport	l'aéroport
bank	la banque
campsite	le camping
pharmacy	la pharmacie
hospital	l'hôpital
police station	la gendarmerie
post office	le bureau de poste
train station	la gare
tourist office	le syndicat d'initiative
youth hostel	l'auberge de jeunesse

Index

bleu	blue	11
blond	blond	11
le blue-jean	jeans	39
le bocal	jar	38
le boeuf	beef	9
boire	to drink	24
le bois	wood	79
la boîte	box	12
bon, bonne	good	33
bon, bonne	kind	39
bon marché	cheap	17
le bonbon	candy	15
le bord	bank	8
le bord	edge	26
la bosse	bump	13
la botte	boot	11
la bouche	mouth	46
le boucher	butcher	14
le bouchon	cork	20
la boue	mud	47
la bougie	candle	15
la bouilloire	kettle	39
le boulanger	baker	7
le bouquet	bunch	13
le bourgeon	bud	13
le bout	end	26
la bouteille	bottle	11
le bouton	button	14
le bracelet	bracelet	12
la branche	branch	12
le bras	arm	6
brillant	bright	12
la brique	brick	12
la brosse	brush	12
la brosse à cheveux	hairbrush	34
la brosse à dents	toothbrush	73
la brouette	wheelbarrow	78
le brouillard	fog	30
le bruit	noise	48
brûler	to burn	13
brun	brown	13
brusquement	suddenly	68
bruyant	loud	44
le buisson	bush	13
le bulbe	bulb	13
le bulldozer	bulldozer	13
la bulle	bubble	13
le bureau	desk	23
le bureau	office	49
la cabane	shed	62
se cacher	hide	36
le cadeau	present	55
le café	café	14
le café	coffee	19
la cage	cage	14
la calculatrice	calculator	15
le calendrier	calendar	15
le cambrioleur	burglar	13
le camion	truck	74
la campagne	country	20
le canapé	sofa	65
le canard	duck	25
la capitale	capital	15
la caravane	trailer	74

le carnet	notebook	48
la carotte	carrot	15
le carré	square	66
le carrefour	intersection	38
le cartable	knapsack	40
la carte	card	15
la carte	map	44
la carte postale	postcard	54
la casquette	cap	15
casser	to break	12
la casserole	pot	55
la cave	cellar	16
la caverne	cave	16
ce, cette, cet, ces	that	71
ce, cette, cet, ces	this	71
la ceinture	belt	9
célèbre	famous	27
le cercle	circle	18
le cerf	deer	22
le cerf-volant	kite	40
la cerise	cherry	17
certain	some	65
la chaîne	chain	16
la chaîne stéréo	stereo	67
la chaise	chair	16
la chambre	bedroom	9
le chameau	camel	15
le champ	field	28
le champignon	mushroom	47
le chandail	sweater	69
changer	to change	16
la chanson	song	65
chanter	to sing	63
le chapeau	hat	35
chaque	each	25
le chat	cat	16
le château	castle	16
le chaton	kitten	40
chaud	warm	77
chaud	hot	37
la chaussette	sock	65
la chaussure	shoe	62
le chef d'orchestre	conductor	20
le chemin	path	51
la cheminée	chimney	17
la chemise	shirt	62
la chenille	caterpillar	16
le chèque	check	17
chercher	to look for	43
le cheval	horse	36
les cheveux (m. pl)	hair	34
la chèvre	goat	33
le chien	dog	23
le chiffre	number	49
le chimpanzé	chimpanzee	17
le chiot	puppy	55
le chocolat	chocolate	17
choisir	to choose	17
la chose	thing	71
le chou	cabbage	14
le chou-fleur	cauliflower	16
chuchoter	to whisper	78
la chute d'eau	waterfall	77
le ciel	sky	64
le cinéma	movie theater	47

cirer	to polish	54
le cirque	circus	18
les ciseaux (m. pl)	scissors	61
le citron	lemon	42
la classe	class	18
la classe	classroom	18
la clé	key	39
le client	customer	21
la cloche	bell	9
la clôture	fence	28
le clou	nail	47
le clown	clown	19
le cochon	pig	53
le coeur	heart	35
le coiffeur	hairdresser	34
le coin	corner	20
le collant	tights	72
le collier	necklace	47
la colline	hill	36
commander	to order	50
commencer	to begin	9
commencer	to start	67
comment	how	37
comprendre	to understand	75
compter	to count	20
le concombre	cucumber	21
conduire	to drive	24
la confiture	jam	38
congeler	to freeze	30
connaître	to know	40
construire	to build	13
content	happy	35
le contraire	opposite	49
contre	against	4
le coq	rooster	59
le coquillage	shell	62
la corde	rope	59
le corps	body	11
le costume	suit	68
la côte	coast	19
le côté	side	63
la côtelette	chop	17
le cou	neck	47
le coude	elbow	26
coudre	to sew	61
la couette	comforter	19
couler	to flow	30
la couleur	color	19
les couleurs (f. pl)	paints	50
la coupe	bowl	11
couper	to cut	21
courir	to run	59
la couronne	crown	21
la course	race	56
court	short	62
le coussin	cushion	21
le couteau	knife	40
coûter	to cost	20
le couvercle	lid	42
la couverture	blanket	10
couvrir	to cover	20
le cowboy	cowboy	20
le crabe	crab	20
la craie	chalk	16
la cravate	tie	72

le crayon	pencil	52
le crayon de couleur	crayon	20
la crème	cream	21
la crêpe	pancake	51
creuser	to dig	23
crier	to yell	80
le crochet	hook	36
le crocodile	crocodile	21
croire	to believe	9
la croix	cross	21
la cruche	pitcher	53
le cube	cube	21
cueillir	to pick	52
la cuiller	spoon	66
le cuir	leather	42
la cuisine	kitchen	40
la cuisinière	stove	68
le cygne	swan	69
le danger	danger	22
dans	in	38
danser	to dance	22
la danseuse	dancer	22
de	from	31
déchirer	to tear	70
décider	to decide	22
découper	to cut out	21
décrire	to describe	22
dehors	outside	50
déjà	already	5
déjeuner	to have lunch	44
demain	tomorrow	73
demander	to ask (for)	7
la dentelle	lace	40
le dentifrice	toothpaste	73
le dentiste	dentist	22
les dents (f. pl)	teeth	70
se dépêcher	to hurry	37
dépenser	to spend	66
déplacer	to move	46
depuis	since	63
dernier, dernière	last	41
derrière	behind	9
des	any	6
le désert	desert	22
déshabiller	to undress	75
le dessin	drawing	24
dessiner	to draw	24
les deux	both	11
devant	in front of	31
les devoirs (m. pl)	homework	36
le diamant	diamond	23
la diapositive	slide	64
le dictionnaire	dictionary	23
différent	different	23
le dîner	dinner	23
le dinosaure	dinosaur	23
dire	to say	60
la direction	direction	23
se disputer	to argue	6
le disque	record	57
le doigt	finger	29
donner	to give	32
donner un coup de pied	to kick	39
dormir	to sleep	64

le dos	back	7	le facteur	mailman	44
la douche	shower	63	faible	weak	77
le dragon	dragon	24	faire	to do	23
le drap	sheet	62	faire	to make	44
le drapeau	flag	29	faire cuire	to fry	31
droit	straight	68	faire la cuisine	to cook	20
droit	right	58	faire du camping	to camp	15
drôle	funny	31	faire du ski	to ski	63
dur	hard	35	faire du voilier	to sail	59
durer	to last	41	faire peur à	to frighten	31
			faire semblant de	to pretend	55
l'eau (f)	water	77	faire un noeud	to tie a knot	72
l'écharpe (f)	scarf	60	la falaise	cliff	18
l'échelle (f)	ladder	40	la famille	family	27
l'éclair (m)	lightning	43	la fanfare	band	8
l'école (f)	school	61	le fantôme	ghost	32
écouter	to listen	43	la farine	flour	30
écrire	to write	80	fatigué	tired	72
l'écriteau (m)	sign	63	le fauteuil	easy chair	25
l'écurie (f)	stable	66	faux, fausse	wrong	80
s'égarer	to be lost	43	la fée	fairy	27
l'église (f)	church	18	la femme	wife	78
l'éléphant (m)	elephant	26	la femme	woman	79
emballer	to wrap	80	la fenêtre	window	79
emporter	to take away	7	le fer à repasser	iron	38
embrasser	to kiss	40	la ferme	farm	28
en	of	49	fermé	shut	63
en bas	downstairs	24	fermer	to close	18
en colère	angry	6	le fermier	farmer	28
en haut	upstairs	75	le feu	fire	29
en retard	late	41	le feu d'artifice	fireworks	29
encore	again	4	le feu de joie	bonfire	11
l'endroit (m)	place	53	la feuille	leaf	41
l'enfant (m)	child	17	les feux (m. pl)	traffic lights	73
ensemble	together	72	la ficelle	string	68
entendre	to hear	35	la figure	face	27
entourer	to surround	69	le fil	thread	71
entre	between	10	le fil de fer	wire	79
l'entrée (f)	entrance	26	la fille	daughter	22
entrer	to enter	26	la fille	girl	32
l'enveloppe (f)	envelope	26	le film	movie	46
envoyer	to send	61	le fils	son	65
épais, épaisse	thick	71	finir	to finish	29
l'épaule (f)	shoulder	62	la flamme	flame	29
épeler	to spell	66	la flèche	arrow	6
l'épicier (m)	grocer	33	la fleur	flower	30
l'épingle (f)	pin	53	le foin	hay	35
épouser	to marry	45	fondre	to melt	45
l'équipe (f)	team	70	le football	soccer	65
escalader	to climb up	18	la forêt	forest	30
l'escalier (m)	stairs	66	la forme	shape	62
l'escargot (m)	snail	65	fort	strong	68
l'espace (m)	space	66	la fourchette	fork	30
l'essence (f)	gasoline	32	la fourmi	ant	6
essuyer	to wipe	79	la fourrure	fur	31
l'est (m)	east	25	la fraise	strawberry	68
et	and	5	la framboise	raspberry	57
étaler	to spread	66	frapper	to hit	36
l'étoile (f)	star	67	frapper	to knock	40
être assis	to sit	63	le frère	brother	12
s'évader	to escape	26	les frites (f. pl)	French fries	31
l'expérience (f)	experiment	27	froid	cold	19
expliquer	to explain	27	le fromage	cheese	17
			le front	forehead	30
facile	easy	25	se frotter	to rub	59

le fruit	fruit	31
fuir	to leak	41
fumer	to smoke	64
gagner	to win	79
le gant	glove	32
le garage	garage	32
le garçon	boy	12
le garçon	waiter	76
garder	to keep	39
la gare	station	67
garer	to park	51
le gâteau	cake	14
gauche	left	42
le gaz	gas	32
le gazon	lawn	41
le géant	giant	32
geler	to freeze	30
le gendarme	policeman	54
le genou	knee	40
les gens (m. pl)	people	52
la girafe	giraffe	32
le givre	frost	31
la glace	ice	37
la glace	ice cream	37
la glace	mirror	45
glisser	to slide	64
goûter	to taste	70
la graine	seed	61
grand	tall	70
grandir	to grow	33
se gratter	to scratch	61
la grenouille	frog	31
gris	gray	33
gros, grosse	big	10
gros, grosse	fat	28
le groupe	group	33
la grue	crane	20
la guêpe	wasp	77
la guerre	war	77
guider	to lead	41
la guitare	guitar	34
habiller	to dress	24
la haie	hedge	35
le hamburger	hamburger	34
le haricot	bean	8
le haut	top	73
haut	high	36
l'hélicoptère (m)	helicopter	35
l'herbe (f)	grass	33
le hérisson	porcupine	54
l'heure (f)	hour	37
le hibou	owl	50
hier	yesterday	80
l'hippopotame (m)	hippopotamus	36
l'histoire (f)	story	68
l'homme (m)	man	44
l'hôpital (m)	hospital	37
l'horloge (f)	clock	18
hors de	out of	50
le hot-dog	hot dog	37
l'hôtel (m)	hotel	37
huiler	to oil	49

ici	here	36
l'idée (f)	idea	37
l'île (f)	island	38
l'imperméable (m)	raincoat	57
important	important	38
l'infirmière (f)	nurse	49
l'insecte (m)	insect	38
intelligent	clever	18
l'invité	guest	33
inviter	to invite	38
la jambe	leg	42
le jambon	ham	34
le jardin	garden	32
jaune	yellow	80
jeter	to throw	72
le jeu	game	31
jeune	young	80
joli	pretty	55
la joue	cheek	17
jouer	to play	54
le jouet	toy	73
le jour	day	22
le journal	newspaper	48
le jumeau, la jumelle	twin	74
la jupe	skirt	64
jusqu'à	until	75
le kangourou	kangaroo	39
là	there	71
le lac	lake	41
laid	ugly	74
la laine	wool	79
la laisse	leash	41
laisser tomber	to drop	24
le lait	milk	45
la laitue	lettuce	42
la lampe	lamp	41
le landau	baby carriage	7
la langue	tongue	73
le lapin	rabbit	56
large	wide	78
la larme	tear	70
le lavabo	sink	63
se laver	to wash	77
le long de	along	5
lécher	to lick	42
la leçon	lesson	42
léger, légère	light	42
le légume	vegetable	76
lentement	slowly	64
la lettre	letter	42
se lever	to get up	32
la lèvre	lip	43
la librairie	bookstore	11
le lion	lion	43
lire	to read	57
la liste	list	43
le lit	bed	9
le livre	book	11
le livre d'exercices	workbook	80
loin	far	28
long, longue	long	43
lorsque	as	7
lourd	heavy	35

la lumière	light	42
la lune	moon	46
les lunettes (f. pl)	glasses	32
la machine	machine	44
la machine à coudre	sewing machine	61
la machine à écrire	typewriter	74
la machine à laver	washing machine	77
le magasin	store	67
maigre	thin	71
le maillot de bain	swimsuit	69
la main	hand	34
maintenant	now	48
mais	but	14
la maison	house	37
malade	ill	38
le malade	patient	51
la manche	sleeve	64
manger	to eat	25
le manteau	coat	19
le marché	market	44
la marche	step	67
la mare	pond	54
le mari	husband	37
le mariage	wedding	77
le marié	bridegroom	12
la mariée	bride	12
le marin	sailor	60
la marionnette	puppet	55
le marteau	hammer	34
le masque	mask	45
le matin	morning	46
mauvais	bad	7
mauvais	rough	59
mécontent	unhappy	75
le médecin	doctor	23
le médicament	medicine	45
le meilleur, la meilleure	best	10
même	same	60
le menton	chin	17
le menu	menu	45
la mer	sea	61
la mère	mother	46
le merle	blackbird	10
mesurer	to measure	45
le métal	metal	45
le métro	subway	68
mettre	to put	56
le miel	honey	36
mieux	better	10
le milieu	middle	45
le minibus	van	75
la minute	minute	45
le modèle réduit	model	46
moelleux, moelleuse	soft	65
le mois	month	46
la moitié	half	34
le monde	world	80
la monnaie	change	16
le monstre	monster	46
la montagne	mountain	46
monter	to go up	75
monter	to ride	58
la montre	watch	77
montrer	to show	63

montrer du doigt	to point	54
le morceau	piece	53
mordre	to bite	10
mort	dead	22
le mot	word	79
la moto	motorcycle	46
la mouche	fly	30
le mouchoir	handkerchief	34
mouillé	wet	77
le moulin à vent	windmill	79
mourir	to die	23
la moustache	mustache	47
le mouton	sheep	62
le mur	wall	76
la musique	music	47
nager	to swim	69
le navire	ship	62
ne … jamais	never	48
ne … personne	nobody	48
neiger	to snow	65
nettoyer	to clean	18
le nez	nose	48
la niche	doghouse	24
le nid	nest	48
Noël	Christmas	18
le noeud	knot	40
noir	black	10
la noix	nut	49
le nom	name	47
le nord	north	48
nourrir	to feed	28
la nourriture	food	30
nouveau, nouvelle	new	48
le nuage	cloud	19
la nuit	night	48
occupé	busy	14
l'oeil, les yeux (m)	eye, eyes	27
l'oeuf (m)	egg	26
offrir	to offer	49
l'oie (f)	goose	33
l'oignon (m)	onion	49
l'oiseau (m)	bird	10
l'ombre (f)	shadow	61
l'oncle (m)	uncle	75
l'or (m)	gold	33
l'orage (m)	storm	67
orange	orange	50
l'orange (f)	orange	50
l'ordinateur (m)	computer	19
l'oreille (f)	ear	25
l'oreiller (m)	pillow	53
l'orteil (m)	toe	72
l'os (m)	bone	11
oser	to dare	22
ou	or	50
où	where	78
oublier	to forget	30
l'ouest (m)	west	77
l'ours (m)	bear	8
l'ours en peluche (m)	teddy bear	70
l'outil (m)	tool	73
ouvert	open	49
ouvrir	to open	49

French	English	Page	French	English	Page
la page	page	50	pincer	to pinch	53
le pain	bread	12	la pipe	pipe	53
la paire	pair	50	le pique-nique	picnic	52
le palais	palace	51	la piscine	swimming pool	69
le pamplemousse	grapefruit	33	le pistolet	gun	34
le panier	basket	8	le placard	cupboard	21
le pantalon	pants	51	le plafond	ceiling	16
la pantoufle	slipper	64	la plage	beach	8
le papier	paper	51	la plaisanterie	joke	39
le papier peint	wallpaper	76	le plancher	floor	29
le papillon	butterfly	14	la plante	plant	53
Pâques (f. pl)	Easter	25	planter	to plant	53
le paquet	package	50	le plat	dish	23
par	through	72	plat	flat	29
par-dessus	over	50	plein	full	31
le parachute	parachute	51	pleurer	to cry	21
le parapluie	umbrella	74	pleuvoir	to rain	57
le parc	park	51	plier	to bend	10
parce que	because	9	la plume	feather	28
les parents (m. pl)	parents	51	la plupart	most	46
paresseux, euse	lazy	41	plus	more	46
parler	to speak	66	le pneu	tire	72
parmi	among	5	la poche	pocket	54
partager	to share	62	la poêle	frying pan	31
partout	everywhere	27	la poire	pear	52
le passeport	passport	51	le poisson	fish	29
se passer	to happen	35	la poitrine	chest	17
passer devant	to pass	51	le poivre	pepper	52
passionnant	exciting	27	poli	polite	54
patiner	to skate	63	la pomme	apple	6
la patte	paw	51	la pomme de terre	potato	55
pauvre	poor	54	le pompier	fireman	29
payer	to pay	52	le poney	pony	54
le pays	country	20	le pont	bridge	12
la peau	skin	64	le porc	pork	54
la pêche	peach	52	le port	harbor	35
pêcher à la ligne	to fish	29	le port	port	54
le peigne	comb	19	la porte	door	24
se peigner	to comb	19	le porte-monnaie	purse	55
peindre	to paint	50	porter	to wear	77
la pelle	shovel	63	porter	to carry	16
pendant que	while	78	le porteur	bellboy	9
penser	to think	71	la poste	post office	54
le père	father	28	la poubelle	garbage can	32
le perroquet	parrot	51	le pouce	thumb	72
peser	to weigh	77	le pouding	pudding	55
petit	small	64	la poule	hen	36
le petit déjeuner	breakfast	12	le poulet	chicken	17
le petit pois	pea	52	la poupée	doll	24
peu	few	28	pour	for	30
peut-être	perhaps	52	pourquoi	why	78
la phare	lighthouse	43	poursuivre	to chase	16
les phares (f. pl)	headlights	35	pousser	to push	56
la pharmacie	drugstore	24	la poussière	dust	25
le phoque	seal	61	le poussin	chick	17
la photo	photograph	52	premier, ière	first	29
la phrase	sentence	61	prendre	to make	70
le piano	piano	52	près de	near	47
la pièce	coin	19	presque	almost	5
la pièce	room	58	le prestidigitateur	magician	44
les pieds (m. pl)	feet	28	le prix	price	55
la pierre	stone	67	le prix	prize	55
la pieuvre	octopus	49	le professeur	teacher	70
la pile	pile	53	profond	deep	22
le pilote	pilot	53	la promenade	walk	76

promettre	to promise	55
propre	clean	18
puis	then	71
puisque	since	63
le puzzle	puzzle	56
le pyjama	pyjamas	56
quand	when	78
que	what	78
quel, quelle	which	78
quelqu'un	anybody	6
quelqu'un	someone	65
quelque chose	something	65
quelquefois	sometimes	65
la question	question	56
la queue	tail	69
qui	who	78
quitter	to leave	42
la racine	root	59
raconter	to tell	70
le radiateur	radiator	56
la radio	radio	56
le raisin	grape	33
ramasser	to pick up	52
ramer	to row	59
la rangée	row	59
se rappeler de	to remember	58
le rasoir	razor	57
le rat	rat	57
rater	to miss	45
rayé	striped	68
recevoir	to receive	57
reconnaître	to recognize	58
le réfrigérateur	refrigerator	57
refuser	to refuse	57
regarder	to look at	43
la reine	queen	56
remercier	to thank	71
remplir	to fill	29
le renard	fox	30
rencontrer	to meet	45
rendre visite à	to visit	76
réparer	to fix	29
repasser	to iron	38
la réponse	answer	4
se reposer	to rest	58
le requin	shark	62
respirer	to breathe	12
rester	to stay	67
le réveil	alarm clock	5
se réveiller	to wake up	76
rêver	to dream	24
la revue	magazine	44
riche	rich	58
le rideau	curtain	21
rien	nothing	48
rire	to laugh	41
la rivière	river	58
le riz	rice	58
la robe	dress	24
le robinet	faucet	28
le rocher	rock	58
le roi	king	39
rond	round	59

rose	pink	53
la rose	rose	59
la roue	wheel	78
rouge	red	57
la route	road	58
le ruban	ribbon	58
la rue	street	68
rugir	to roar	58
le ruisseau	stream	58
le sable	sand	60
le sac	bag	7
le sac	sack	59
le sac à main	handbag	34
sain et sauf	safe	59
la salade	salad	60
sale	dirty	23
la salle à manger	dining room	23
la salle de bains	bathroom	8
le salon	living room	43
la sandale	sandal	60
le sandwich	sandwich	60
le sang	blood	11
sans	without	79
la sauce	sauce	60
la saucisse	sausage	60
sauf	except	27
sauter	to jump	39
sauter	to hop	36
savoir	to know	40
le savon	soap	65
la scie	saw	60
le seau	bucket	13
sec, sèche	dry	25
secouer	to shake	62
le sel	salt	60
sembler	to seem	61
sentir	to smell	64
le serpent	snake	65
la serviette	towel	73
servir	to serve	61
se servir de	to use	75
seul	alone	5
seulement	only	49
le short	shorts	62
si	if	38
le sifflet	whistle	78
silencieusement	quietly	56
le singe	monkey	46
le ski	ski	64
la soeur	sister	63
le soir	evening	26
le sol	ground	33
le soldat	soldier	65
le soleil	sun	69
la solution	answer	6
sombre	dark	22
sonner	to ring	58
la sorcière	witch	79
la sorte	kind	39
la sorte	sort	65
la soucoupe	saucer	60
souffler	to blow out	11
soulever	to lift	42
la soupe	soup	66

sourire	to smile	64	travailler	to work	79
la souris	mouse	46	traverser	to cross	21
sous	under	75	très	very	76
le sous-marin	submarine	68	le trésor	treasure	74
se souvenir de	to remember	58	le triangle	triangle	74
souvent	often	49	le tricot	knitting	40
la statue	statue	67	tricoter	to knit	40
le stylo	pen	52	triste	sad	59
le sucre	sugar	68	la trompette	trumpet	74
le sud	south	66	trop	too	73
suivre	to follow	30	le trottoir	sidewalk	63
le supermarché	supermarket	69	le trou	hole	36
sur	about	4	trouver	to find	29
sur	on	49	tuer	to kill	39
la surprise	surprise	69	la tulipe	tulip	74
la surprise-partie	party	51			
suspendre	to hang	34	l'usine (f)	factory	27
			utile	useful	75
la table	table	69			
le tableau	picture	52	les vacances (f. pl)	vacation	75
le tableau noir	blackboard	10	la vache	cow	20
le tablier	apron	6	la vague	wave	77
la tache	mark	44	la valise	suitcase	69
la tache	spot	66	la vallée	valley	75
le tambour	drum	25	le vase	vase	76
la tante	aunt	7	le veau	calf	15
taper à la machine	to type	74	vendre	to sell	61
le tapis	carpet	15	venir	to come	19
tard	late	41	le vent	wind	79
la tasse	cup	21	le ver de terre	worm	80
le taureau	bull	13	le verre	glass	32
le taxi	taxi	70	vers	towards	73
le téléphone	telephone	70	verser	to pour	55
la télévision	television	70	vert	green	33
tenir	to hold	36	la veste	jacket	38
se tenir debout	to stand	66	la viande	meat	45
le tennis	tennis	71	vide	empty	26
la tente	tent	71	vider	to empty	26
la terre	earth	25	la vie	life	42
la tête	head	35	vieux, vieille	old	49
le thé	tea	70	vilain	naughty	47
le théâtre	theater	71	le village	village	76
la théière	teapot	70	la ville	city	18
la tige	stem	67	la ville	town	73
le tigre	tiger	72	violet	purple	56
le timbre	stamp	66	le violon	violin	76
tirer	to pull	55	vite	fast	28
la toile d'araignée	cobweb	19	la vitre	window	79
le toit	roof	58	vivre	to live	43
la tomate	tomato	72	voici	here is	36
tomber	to fall	27	voici	this is	72
tôt	early	25	la voie ferrée	railroad track	56
toucher	to touch	73	voilà	that is	71
toucher	to feel	28	voir	to see	61
toujours	always	5	la voiture	car	15
la tour	tower	73	la voix	voice	76
tourner	to turn	74	voler	to fly	30
la tourte	pie	53	voler	to steal	67
tous, toutes	all	5	le voleur	thief	71
tous, toutes	every	26	vouloir	to want	76
tousser	to cough	20	vrai	real	57
tout	everything	27			
tout le monde	everyone	27	les yeux (m. pl)	eyes	27
le tracteur	tractor	73			
le train	train	74	le zèbre	zebra	80
la tranche	slice	64	le zoo	zoo	80